The art of not disappearing

Dr Vangjel Shore

RIVER
PUBLISHING

River Publishing & Media Ltd
Barham Court
Teston
Maidstone
Kent
ME18 5BZ
United Kingdom

info@river-publishing.co.uk

Scripture quotations are taken from various Bible versions listed in the bibliography

ISBN 978-1-908393-11-1

Printed in the United Kingdom

Contents

Dedication

This, my first book, is dedicated to my wife, Heazle.
She is the only angel I have ever met.
She has loved the best and the worst about me and
inspires me to live life out of the box!

Foreword

I first met Van on the Gold Coast of Australia. After a talk I had given we spoke in the food queue. I instantly liked him and I still do! Since then I have come to know and love the man of revelation, his integrity and passion for life and God – all married with a unique and deep spirituality which is a delight to drink from and be with.

I have enjoyed many memorable, inspirational conversations with Van, spiced with quotations and insights from a broad spectrum of literature and sprinkled with his poetic language, pictures and one-liners. Here is one of them: "God is an interior decorator; He starts from the inside out."

This book, in part, is the experiential proof that Van knows what he is talking about. He is the most healed "damaged person" I have ever met. This insightful and different book is well worth the read. It will inspire you, challenge you, ask you questions, give you answers and above all focus you on Jesus.

You will probably be disarmed by his vulnerability in the telling of his story. I pray you will be drawn into God's deeper magic by the challenge of walking with God and know the emancipating freedom of "just being yourself". For me, the discovery that I am not truly human – authentically who God made me to be – without knowing that I am only adequate when I see my inadequacy without God and those He deliberately placed on the pathway of life, has been a shocking revelation.

I can still remember the setting of my first hearing of Van's "VTR" message, referred to later in this book. It "stripped me" then as it does now, as I reflect upon it again. What does it truly look like to "Come, follow me?" I could go on, but I must stop! You must turn the page and capture the jewels on the pages ahead. But one final thought: it has been well said, "Always start with the end in mind." Well, the end of this book is about meeting God "face to face", so please hear Him saying to you through every page you read, ever so loving but ever so clear: "Look at me when I speak to you." Please do!

David Shearman
Nottingham,
September 2011

"In reality, every reader while he is reading finds himself. The writer's work is merely a kind of optical instrument that makes it possible for a reader to discern what, without this book, he would perhaps never have seen in himself."
(Marcel Proust, 1871-1922)

Introduction

Self-disclosure can be a pretty scary thing. In fact, it can also be very painful. However, if it inspires and informs then truly nothing is ever wasted. In 2009 my wife and I were in Cambodia. It was our thirty-third wedding anniversary. I asked God to tell me what I had learned from my wife throughout our married life. The response or impression which I received was almost immediate: *Heazle has taught you how to not disappear.* I was startled and disturbed. Precisely what that expression meant is the impetus for the creation of the book that is in your hands.

I am more than sure that many of us, when we were growing up, enjoyed playing the game "hide and seek". It is a fun game. For children, their exploits in hiding are short lived, because they know that it is only a game. Furthermore, there is the added excitement of being found. But have you ever thought just how much adults continue with this game throughout much of their lives?

For many, "hide and seek" is a daily engagement – no longer a fun game designed to amuse – and the motivation for it is driven by something far deeper and more powerful – fear. We hide from others because we fear self-disclosure and the vulnerability that intimacy with others brings.

This is precisely why the impression, "Heazle has taught you how to not disappear" struck a chord deep within me. A friend reminded me that all of us experience such "light bulb moments" in life – when a truth is suddenly illuminated and we see like we have never seen before. Our "seeing" is not so much about the world around us, but the world within us. It is my prayer that in reading this book, you will have a similar "light bulb" moment.

History's very first "hide and seekers" were Adam and Eve - in fact they invented the game. They wilfully disobeyed God and found themselves suddenly exposed, vulnerable and guilty. Their first response was to try to cover up what they'd done and hide from God. But God came to seek them out.

Not only was God intent on finding them – He wanted them to truly find Him.

This is still God's heart for us today. He desires to find us and to skill us in *the art of not disappearing*. This is a way of living lost to so many. For all our modern progressive attitudes and sophistication, we have become skilled in hiding not just from God and others, but especially from ourselves.

Therefore, it is my sincere prayer that every page of this book will provide for you a rich and very personal insight into who God is and what you truly mean to Him. I hope it will help you to better understand who you are and where your story fits into God's story.

My appeal in the first chapter is to challenge us to stop and recapture with freshness of insight the need to examine the well-worn, familiar expression: Once upon a time...

We all have a story, a history. But that story does not need to dictate or dominate the shape of our future in Christ. My early years were largely characterised by bold strokes of tragedy, disillusionment and self-destructive behaviour. However, I am committed to the liberating truth of the opening words of the Hebrew Scriptures: *"In the beginning God created..."* (Genesis 1:1). These words are liberating. They tell us that no matter what has transpired in our life, God was there at the very beginning and will be there at all our beginnings.

The second chapter, *God's Deeper Magic*, invites us to experience and explore just how much God is already involved in our lives, long before we ever acknowledge His existence. In cleverly disguised dress, God comes often into our lives. He comes to us, up close and personal, through friends and so often through people who we have little to do with. What a profound difference it can make when we discover that God has been working His deeper magic in our lives for a very long time. Purposefully, His intention all along was to include us in His bigger story. God has always intended to enrich and enlarge, empower and energise us to truly live out our own story.

The third chapter relates to a very defining moment for me, which I call, "The Day the Image Shattered". I was disillusioned and disenchanted in many areas of my life. In an attitude of prayer, I was confronted with a picture on the screen of my imagination. The aftermath of what transpired was overwhelming. The picture God provided had done its work on me, resulting in the acquisition of valuable wisdom and provocative insights.

The fourth chapter allows us to discover that when our story is placed within the narrative of Jesus' story, then we are no longer consigned to the previous scripts of our lives. It is this discovery which will, I believe, cause each of us to know that the William Wallace cry of "Freedom!" from the film *Braveheart* can be ours. Yet wonderfully, not at the end of our life, but with every new beginning that God wants to give to us. This new found freedom to live according to God's script is all due to what Jesus Christ has done and will do for you.

Finally, the fifth chapter, *Meeting God Face to Face*, is intended to draw each of us into the only place where we may truly know that we no longer have to hide our faces; the place where each of us can know that we can *live life loved*.

This place – the presence of God – is where, throughout the centuries, millions of people have experienced the exchange of beauty for their ashes and the oil of joy for their deep mourning. This place cannot be experienced through the earnest efforts of humanity. It is the place where, all along, God has chosen to reveal His face to us. Indeed, it is only when we can look into His face, that we truly have a "face".

By drawing upon the challenges of life-experience and biblical insights it is my conviction that this book will provide an unvarnished approach to what it means to be your true self. The title itself is intended to call us out and into that very precious place of learning to accept the person God has always intended us to be. The simplicity of these chapters is designed to encourage you to:

• accept that as with all stories, including our own, each begins with a Once Upon a Time... yet the script is neither iron clad nor the final word on your life
• be honest with the darkness and the light
• know the God who you thought you knew, maybe for the first time
• appreciate why love is so important from the beginning to the end in our very human journey with Jesus
• simply stay in love with Jesus
• experience God's self-disclosure to you, Face to face, and,
• inspire in you the courage to believe that God's love will not only never let you go, but will never let you get away with anything that could sabotage His work in making you, *you!*

"...the child who has experienced no validation of his or her ideals and ambitions has nothing but an opaque mirror. Without mirroring, there can be no self; the light of self depends on the mirroring it receives from without."

(Donald Capps)

1
Once Upon a Time...

After some twenty plus years in pastoral ministry, working closely with people and helping them to make sense of their stories, it is time for me to tell my own story. Therefore, I want to draw out of the scrapbook of my memories a specific incident which was essentially the defining moment in my life. It was this specific incident which made up the raw material of who I am and what I have become, both as a person and, professionally, as a pastor and a teacher. Even though this incident occurred in my life as an eight-year old, the repercussions invariably shaped the way I saw myself, others, the world in which I lived, and especially the way I related to God. I could never have imagined how far-reaching the shadow of this incident would be. It certainly dominated my life and, on the face of it, forever shaped the script of my life from those earliest years.

I have often heard it said that in the entertainment industry the motivation for the majority of aspiring actors is to reach the place where they are free to choose their own scripts – to be no longer caught in the never-ending characterisations and diverse roles that help to eke out an existence until the "big break" comes. The big break is when, "I can be me and appreciated for who I am."

As much as this notion is true for the entertainment industry, equally, a similar desire drives each of us. We have an inherent longing to be our true selves with no covering up, appreciated for who we are and not merely for the roles we have to play on a daily basis. We long for our "performance" not to be the criteria with which our worth and value as a person is measured.

I have often reflected on that critical moment when we leave the world of the womb to the moment of our entry into this world. In effect, a script is already being played out. We are plunged, if not catapulted, into a world alive with characters, which we are either attracted to or repelled by. We meet a world characterised by unfamiliar faces, voices, sounds and a whole lot more than we could have ever imagined.

It is a bit like walking into a cinema halfway through a movie. Immediately, we are struck with a sense of confusion on many fronts. We have absolutely no idea what is going on, let alone what has taken place up to this point in the movie. Almost everything appearing before our eyes is somewhat sketchy and vague. Bits and pieces of the movie begin to impose their presence on us. Characters speak, but the content of their conversations remain elusive and enigmatic.

However, deep down, even though we are feeling drawn into this story, a growing suspicion is aroused toward each character. Quite remarkably, attraction and repulsion make their presence felt. We feel strangely attracted to the story and its characters. Some of the characters not only arouse a sense of discomfort, but also make us downright scared. Nevertheless, there is a recognition that each one has their place in the story. Perhaps the most disturbing aspect of this experience is that we feel like we should know what this story is about, or at least where it is going.

To be blunt, the early beginnings of our story have absolutely nothing to do with you or me. Our story commences without us having any real say as to how it is going to begin and end, let alone what will necessarily transpire in between. Even more imposing is the stark reality that the many characters in our imaginary movie – those we liked and those we found it hard to cope with – are already in *our* story. These characters represent parents, siblings, relatives and, of course, all the extras who we accumulate and gather along the way.

In the telling of my own story, a brief qualification is necessary. I have very little recollection of "Infancy, Early Childhood or Play Age" due to traumatic experiences. Of that which I do remember, the phrase that most aptly describes my earliest childhood memory would have to be chaotic upheaval. The locality is home. A myriad of images confront me with the same message: *life is basically disappointing*. This message about life resonated with me up until the age of twenty-five. From then on, this belief regarding the unsatisfactory nature of life was no longer tenaciously held, nor would it dictate my tomorrows. If your past argues with your present, then there is really very little to look forward to regarding the future. However, first things first, let me introduce you to my parents and family.

In the shadow of my father

I really didn't get to know my father until much later on in life. In fact, it was a few days before his seventieth birthday when this truth became so apparent to both of us. Telling out that aspect of the story awaits the second chapter of this book. The story will confront you, the reader, with the events which were so momentous and life-changing for both of us.

As far back as I can recall, I had always had a very unsettled and nervous disposition towards my father. The most dominant feature of my relationship with him was ambivalence. I was impaled on the horns of a love-hate relationship. I always wanted to please him, but was never able to do so. My father had no problem in projecting self-contempt onto others. His contempt for himself was very much related to his drinking bouts. His violent and abusive ways towards my mother and the rest of my family were a constant. He was, in the words of Donald Capps, the paranoid type of narcissist – a person who is, "...hypersensitive, jealous, envious, [who has] unwarranted suspicion and a tendency to blame others and ascribe evil motives to them."

This description comprehensively depicted my father. In addition, his vicious criticism of me was harsh and demanding. If my father was a paranoid-narcissist, then conversely, I was the craving-narcissist – emotionally starved and expecting disappointment.

As a child, it was not an uncommon sight to see my mother enduring both physical and emotional abuse. My father would hurl expletives at her with recurring frequency. Images of drunkenness, accompanied by volatile obscenities, frequent beatings and untold accusations would force me to retreat into hiding. Three places visibly stand out as my places of refuge: under a bed, in a wardrobe or in a small dark corner under the house.

Strange as it may seem, hiding under my parents' bed deepened my desire to be near them – especially my mother. I felt every invective of the harsh, abusive tongue of my father's whip-like words towards her. I so wanted to protect her and be close enough for her. Whether she knew I was there or not, I was never sure.

Either way, it mattered to me to be there. I desperately wanted to be able to turn on my father and reduce him to putty to be mashed up. He was so cruel and such a bully. But as an eight-year old I had resigned myself to being totally powerless and therefore of no use to my mother or, for that matter, anyone else. These are huge calls to make as an eight year old. They invariably took their toll.

But hiding away in the wardrobe provided me with a whole other world. Once I was in, I entertained myself with a host of imaginary characters – characters who I could speak to and play with. I felt safe. I never derived anything harmful from these characters, though I was always keenly aware that I craved their company in my darkness and pain, my isolation and grief. My third place of safety – the small dark corner under the house – merely provided me with the physical space to be hidden from everyone.

Hiding under the bed or in the wardrobe only served to heighten and intensify the activities of the adult world – namely that I was totally unable to change anything or anyone, so I would be better off staying put in the darkness. Similarly, the dark corner of the house was etched in my memory as the place for brooding and fermenting the wine of my deep discontent. All the time I had absolutely no idea that by escaping to these places, I was actually training myself in the art of disappearing.

Tension was a constant in the home. It was more often a war zone, with each family member suffering from battle fatigue. Absenteeism from the war zone was a given for my older brothers. The very thought of conflict resolution was as foreign as me trying to stand up to my father or brothers and telling them, "We need to change the way we relate and behave towards each other." When we were there with each other, we were so much not there for each other. Confrontation was always about who had the loudest voice in order to dominate everyone else or, conversely, who would acquiesce to withdrawal and resolve to simply shut up. Conflict resolution was never on the agenda.

Survival and coexistence were the operative words which shaped those early years for all of us. As my brothers got older, their lives became enmeshed in their own interests. Home was merely a place to stay – it was not an environment conducive to becoming persons with faces and names, loved and affirmed by all who lived there. My father continued his haphazard lifestyle and, over many days, weeks, months and years, I adopted the image of Dostoyevsky's, "...underground man who had seen too much and walled it off, unable to forgive ... yet who must live with the source of his rage and spite."

Living with my father was an arduous effort of contending with ambivalence. On the one hand, hatred had filled my heart. On the other hand, some sort of notion of guilt pierced me deeply. I carried within me a peculiar sense of aspiration that I could be a good son who would not get in his way. I also carried within my heart an even deeper secret that just one day he might tell me that he loved me. If, as I believe, hope is the memory of a future, then hope was clearly absent or deeply blurred from my heart and mind, even from day one.

How very sad that I had been brought into a home which was not a home; into a world dominated by language charged with abuse in many and varied forms. The language of my home, whether spoken or unspoken, was destructive on all fronts. Small morsels of affirming words of love from my mother and father and family members were generally conspicuously absent. Yet, when they came I would surely devour them. Like a heroin addict hanging out for his next fix, I too was hanging out for my next fix of affirmation and love.

I was afraid of my father and I felt so alone. Even though I had convinced myself that the walls which I had built within me were impenetrable, somehow my father's words and actions would always hit the target. I would be left wounded inside. If ever he stretched out his hands towards me, it was not a moment of embrace; rather, it was a moment to recoil from. His drinking habit only caused me to laugh at him. I lived my life on a seesaw playing out the rhythm of *I love you and I hate you* with nothing much in between. The constancy of these ups and the downs strongly shaped my early years. I had convinced myself that I could never make it in my father's eyes. Worst of all, self-hatred began to set in and take its toll on my life. Consequently, I did not even "make it" in my own eyes. My father was larger than life. Before him, I felt so terribly small and insignificant

When it came to school days, these were quite clumsy and awkward. Inferiority dominated the horizon of my life. I was suspicious of teachers, parents and students. In order to address my awkwardness, I would either play up and behave badly or be quiet and introverted. Both of these were extreme sports. Playing games with others was more about manipulation and staying at the centre of attention. At worst, these were sheer survival skills I would practice on others until they grew tired of me and left me alone.

I had hosted many a pity party, a carryover of my upbringing. Either way, I sought to "disappear" so that I would never allow anyone to find me. Sure, I was physically present in the home and in the classroom, yet absent from everyone by brooding in my own cavernous world. On a daily basis I felt that my life was inescapably determined by my father. Inwardly, I was haunted by the never ending lament, *I do not want to be like you, Dad.* Enter my mother and sister...

Before the day ends

Already you have gained some insight into my father. Earlier I made mention of traumatic experiences that have affected my ability to recall the earlier years of my childhood. This is where my mother had figured so prominently. Both of my parents were Albanian. My mother had married in her early teens to my father. They fled Albania before Communism overthrew the government. Life in Australia offered the prospects of a new start for many Albanians. For my father and mother, Brisbane was their new home. Four children were born: three boys and a girl.

I was the youngest child. My relationship with my mother was inextricably linked with Rhonda, my sister. Rhonda would often read and play with me. Her imagination inspired me to dream and fantasise. Hence, my places of refuge – the bed, the wardrobe and the small dark corner under the house – merely became the laboratory for all my experimentation with fantasy. Apart from Rhonda, fantasy was my closest friend. I had conceived many imaginative characters and never once was Rhonda dismissive of any one of them. She read, she played and she enjoyed being with me. Rhonda was like a second mum to me. Rhonda would hardly ever talk about dad and she would often try to help mum around the home. My father would often say to Rhonda, "You will learn what wives are for." However, for Rhonda, the opportunity to ever be a wife would never become a reality. Tragically, she died when she was eleven years old – and in the most tragic way imaginable.

The events of that particular day began, as per usual, with the daily ritual of having breakfast. We were all together, except for my father. He was a chef and would often arrive home in the early hours of the morning or sometimes mid-morning. We were having our breakfast and mum was making the school lunches. An argument had ensued between one of my brothers and Rhonda.

My mother intervened in the heated exchange. The next thing I knew was that my mother had stabbed Rhonda in the chest with the bread knife. The knife was very sharp. Blood went everywhere and panic ensued. I am not entirely sure about the timing of the events that followed, but as an eight-year old little boy I fled to a familiar place – hiding in that small, dark corner under the house. All alone and very scared, I crouched in the dark. I could hear my mother calling out to my brothers to help her. They carried Rhonda into the bathroom, laid her in the bathtub, and attempted to stem the flow of blood. However, by the time the ambulance had arrived, Rhonda had lost a huge amount of blood.

My dad arrived home at virtually the same time as the police. He shouted at my mother: "You have murdered Rhonda; you have killed her!" He vented the full force of his anger upon her and then turned to my brothers, yelling at them and beginning to wrestle with them. The police intervened and subdued Dad. I witnessed the entire, terrible incident. My brothers and my father were all out in the front yard. Through the ventilation slat, I saw Rhonda being carried out on a stretcher. Under the escort of a policewoman, my mother followed. Two policemen accompanied my father and my brothers. The neighbours had also gathered to bear witness to these tragic events. It was terrifying.

Relatively speaking, the memories of that day have remained somewhat inaccessible to me. Intentionally or unintentionally, locking them away in my subconscious allowed me to survive the years to come. The operative verb for me was *survive*.

Nevertheless, the one thing that characterised that day is the feeling of absolute despair which only a helpless eight-year old child can ever know. A myriad of images and sounds were indelibly impressed upon me for years and years. The images...

- of Rhonda's crumpled body slumped over the kitchen table
- Rhonda's blood on my shirt, as I was the nearest person to her
- my mother gasping for breath, choking on the pain
- seeing her eyes filled with the horror and dread of what she had done
- Mum's body becoming lifeless, as if struck down and rendered powerless to the force of the impending disaster
- the panic and fear in everyone's eyes

And the sounds...

- of the dull thud of the knife hitting Rhonda's chest
- of my mother's distraught cries, "No, no, no! What have I done?"
- of my mother shaking like a child having an epileptic fit
- and her deep uncontrollable sobbing

As scared as I was, so alone, so utterly vulnerable, I did what I always did. I hid. This incident would somehow signify my relationship with my mother, father and my brothers and my world – outwardly existing, yet inwardly determined to remain hidden and untouchable. This was so close to the truth. I had been penetrated and marked by this incident at a level much deeper and far more profoundly that an eight-year old could ever want or even imagine.

Rhonda's stabbing and her tragic, untimely death accentuated for each family member that we had been separated from each other. We were never really together as one in the first place. The loss of Rhonda had only further magnified the reality of just how much death had already made inroads into the very fabric of our family prior to this unspeakable tragedy. Death is so much more than the demise of a person's life. It forcibly confronts us with the total *absence* of life. As a family we had been enslaved to habits and patterns of behaviour which neither nourished nor engendered a quality of life that would allow each of us to know love and affirmation. Our conversations were upheld mostly by small talk. The fleeting glances we gave one another merely confirmed that we were more like ships passing in the night.

After the incident, a policeman kept calling out my name. Because my hiding place was so small, the policeman was prevented from being able to reach me. My insides were bursting. I was screaming out, *Please come and find me.* Yet I did not want to be found. A new dimension had interrupted my life. It came as an unexpected intruder. This death was unlike any other. I had been to the funerals of relatives, but this was Rhonda, my sister, my playmate, my teacher, my imaginary characters' closest friend and my surrogate mother. It was like a thousand deaths all at once. She was bleeding, she was hurting and then she was gone. Death was so final. Death does not have to wait until people are elderly. Indeed, death is no respecter of persons. In my young life the script was already firmly in place that life was thoroughly disappointing. Quite literally, this hit me out of the ballpark. I would never be the same again.

Like an endless falling

My mother was sent to prison where she would be incarcerated for a long time for what was regarded as a "violent death". My aunt recently reminded me that after some period of time, my mother was allowed out on weekends. These were onerously awkward for all concerned. No one knew what to do or how to respond to her.

Then she would simply return to her cell. My father's drinking had escalated and he withdrew from everyone. Much of his time had been spent visiting the graveside of Rhonda. My father avoided visiting his wife and his absence, I am sure, further reinforced her deepening sense of shame. As a family we were sent to live with relatives – precariously living out an existence which would never again galvanize, in any healthy sense of the word, what it means to be a family. We were cared for and yet strangely aware that conversations regarding the events of that tragic day were not to be discussed. An ominous silence was more than evident in all our social circles. Shame, shame, shame, was the characteristic feature associated with my mother and the tragic event.

I can't speak on behalf of my father or my brothers, but for me, I had encountered multiple losses: the loss of my mother; the absence of my father (who in many ways was already lost to me); Rhonda's terrible death and my loss of connection with my brothers.

If I had had to explain to someone exactly what each member of my family experienced that day, my response, for many years, would have been that the story remained untold. None of them ever spoke of such things – that is until many years later. At the age of fifty-seven, I vividly recall a visit overseas with my brother in 2007. I had travelled from Brazil to Auckland. I arrived very early in the morning. We had not seen each other for a number of years. We met at the airport and embraced.

He took me to his home and showed me to my room and said that I should sleep after such a long flight. I was elated and so excited that I wanted to stay up and catch up on every conceivable subject which related to our lives as brothers. I was like a child left alone in a confectionary store. Before I went to sleep, he came in with a present for me. It was a large picture frame and enclosed was a photo of us as children. I would have been about four, perhaps five years old. I was absolutely motionless. I gazed at it and studied each face, especially Rhonda's. I could not hold myself together. I fell apart. I was well and truly undone. I had said to my brother that I remembered hiding in the corner under the old house for a few hours. He reminded me that I was actually under the house for a whole day and well into the evening. I just would not come out.

Worse still, my brother James, with tears in his eyes, immediately said, "I cannot talk about this, it is much too painful." That was the end of the conversation. I cried myself to sleep. The new day dawned, but I knew that I could not resurrect the topic of the preceding day. I had to respect my brother's wishes and not demand that he answer the endless questions I had.

As an eight-year old, all that had transpired was like being totally and comprehensively covered from head to toe with pain. It was not the pain of a toothache or a broken limb, though that can certainly make one feel that the whole body is in pain. This was like no other pain I had ever experienced. It transcended the physical. All I knew and felt was a deep sense of abandonment and rejection from every member of my family, especially from Rhonda. It hurt all over.

Thomas Moore has made this rather telling observation regarding family life:

"Family life presents the full range of human potential, including evil, hatred, violence, sexual confusion and, insanity ... a sometimes comforting, a sometimes devastating house of life and memory."

Any notions of comforting memories in my childhood were inevitably swallowed up by the ravenous appetite of the unbearable losses which I had experienced and, quite frankly, had not asked for. The last time that I saw my mother was at Rhonda's funeral. My mother was visibly shaken and had to be supported. The policewoman who was at the house on the morning Rhonda died attended to mum. I kept looking at my mother, almost expecting her to say something to me or do something. I saw someone different. I saw that my mother was a broken person and I could not do anything about it or for her. She was just like me, alone and frightened.

Loud sobs could be heard all over the cathedral. My father did not look good either. I had never seen him this way before. He had always frightened me. Now he appeared fragile and powerless. It seemed that he had been reduced to my level of helplessness. For the very first time, I actually felt bigger and stronger than him. It was weird. I actually indulged myself in a perverted sense of pleasure in being able to see my father reduced to this. My morose attitude and perverse delight towards my father and my mother only confirms for me the capacity of the human heart to manifest gross and distorted power over the very people who are closest to us. There was no compassion on my part. I was just plain angry and sad at what I had lost. I was eight years old; I could not get my head around what had taken place. Now that I am fifty-nine, I have realised that in those days no one ever spoke about their feelings anyway. In fact, a generation was spawned on the ideology that "children are to be seen but never heard".

My brothers were wiping the tears from their faces. Others in the cathedral wiped away their tears, while others simply stared in unbelief and dismay, wondering how such a tragic event could happen. *She was so young and then all of a sudden...* was the subject of the conversations that day. I remained numb. I simply sat in the cathedral, fascinated by the stained glass windows with the images imprinted on the glass and the candles burning. The priest was multilingual, but his English was very broken; Greek was obviously his native tongue. The priest was accompanied by four men who were standing at his side. They were chanting selected scriptures from the gospel of John. There was no music, simply the music of their voices.

My grandmother and aunts, in one accord, said to me, "You must be strong and be brave." Strength and bravery were far from me and whatever those terms meant, I was gone. As much as folk sought to be near me, an emotional distance rose up within me. Strangely enough, I wanted to be near to the very ones who had hurt me so much. And yet, I also wanted to be in my small dark corner or in my wardrobe – anywhere where I could simply disappear. Viktor Frankl aptly comments,

"A man's concern, even in his despair over the worthlessness of life is spiritual distress, but by no means a mental disease."

The tragedy is that the very persons we ought to admire are often those whom we hold in disrespect. According to Donald Capps, this is due to "being deprived of the mirroring that occurs when there is shared admiration, child for parent and, parent for child." Helen Lynd reinforces this:

"The impact of shame for others may reach even deeper than shame for ourselves. This is true not only of shame for our parents, but in very different ways of feeling shame with others."

My insides felt like a crowded house. Resentment and ingratitude, inferiority and shame clung to me like leeches. Inferiority pursued me throughout this stage in my life and onto all the other stages of my life. Little could I have ever realised the import of the shame which accompanied my deepening sense of inferiority. Any real sense of belonging had been severely damaged. Over these days, two factors dominated the horizon of my world. On the one hand, the haunting sense of death had impressed itself upon me and, on the other hand, the collective brooding silence regarding Rhonda's death reinforced in me that it was everyone's awkward attempt at concealing the fact that they too were ashamed of the terrible incident. If not ashamed, perhaps each was enveloped with a strong sense of powerlessness, unable to say the right thing. What does one say anyway? *I have often wondered whether everyone might have a small dark corner where they would go and cry and say stuff out loud?*

Personally, these years proved to be disturbing and quite problematic. My growing resentment towards people became all the more apparent through my gloating over every opportunity to hit out and harm anyone who came into my radar. Much more insidious and much to my chagrin, was my growing predisposition towards punishing both males and females. All males represented the father who I despised, and females represented my mother who I hated because she took Rhonda away from me. And, of course, Rhonda, why would she leave me? Therefore, as I grew into a young man, I had numerous sexual escapades, each of which were very much related to my punitive agenda. Heterosexual and homosexual behaviour had no moral compass as far as I was concerned. Sexual expression was not about relationship and intimacy.

The language of intimacy was one thing; I had digested enough poetry to realise that there was such a thing as intimacy and transparency. But the reality of it was distant from me. As a child, hiding under my parent's bed, I was present when my parents had engaged in lovemaking. It was brutal and harsh. It was all over with so quickly. It was little more than masturbatory behaviour, devoid of the giving of oneself to another. Hence, my understanding of intimacy was largely programmed by such preconditioning.

Throughout my school years, I worked very hard at staying

detached from others. My thirst for knowledge was a bonus, but I flaunted knowledge in such a manner as to seduce people. I firmly believed that I was the one in control. I grew increasingly comfortable wearing the label *Restricted Access Zone*. This way, I could give to others when I felt like it and only on my terms. Conversely, no one could take from me without my consent or permission. I was always on the defensive. Repeatedly, I would play out roles and navigate scripts of my own design. The driving motive was both punitive and fed by the desire to control others.

Sadly and very disturbingly, as I got older, I became acutely aware that I was not in control after all. The shocking realisation for me was that I had been controlled by desires which were twisted and motives which were murkier than any dark or dingy place where my deepest shame had taken me. If it is true that we find our identity through our relationship with another, then the quest for me was to find that "other". We either flourish from someone loving us or we wither from negative mirroring.

Asleep and often inert to the constancy of God's purpose for our lives, none of us are strangers to things falling apart. The amazing fact stands out for me, however, is that the stories of the characters which constituted my fragmented world did not remain the same. The following chapter ushers us into the world of God, a much larger world, and looks into what God would do to change the script which has controlled each of our lives. If my *once upon a time* story has caught your attention, than be prepared to listen further as you encounter *God's Deeper Magic*.

Endnotes:

1. Erikson's life-cycle theory suggests that the "normal human life span consists of eight stages or ages." *Identity and the Life Cycle* (New York:

International Universities Press, 1959), p46.

2. D. Capps, The Depleted Self (Minneapolis: Augsburg Press, 1993), p22.

3. Refer to J. Kovel, A Complete Guide to Therapy (UK: Penguin Books, 1991), p127.

4. See Thomas Moore, The Care of the Soul (New York: Harper and Collins, 1992) pp29-30.

5. Refer to Viktor Frankl, A Man's Search for Meaning, (New York: Washington Square Publications, 1974) p104.

6. See H. Lynd, On Shame and the Search for Identity New York: Harvest Books, 1958) p56.

"Scholarly commentaries on our 'postmodern condition' often make much of our fixation on the surfaces of reality. In such a context it is a good thing to be encouraged to go beyond the superficial, exploring not only the Deeper Magic, but also the other below-the-surface forces which drive our lives, even when we do not acknowledge their existence. Namely, our Deeper Hopes and our Deeper Fears –those Deeper which we ignore at the expense of our humanness."

(Richard Mouw)[1]

2
God's Deeper Magic

If ever I was asked which character in the Bible I would most readily identify with, immediately without hesitation, my response was always the same. It wasn't one of the great heroes of the faith – like Abraham or David – nor one of the prominent leaders in the early Christian community – like Peter, James or John. My immediate response, for a very long time, was Mephibosheth. His story is recorded in in 2 Samuel 9.

Mephibosheth, for most people at least, is not a character known to be successful or even particularly well known in the biblical narrative. However, chief among the many reasons why I could so readily identify with this man, was the meaning of his name – which according to Eugene Peterson means "Seething Dishonour".[2] Furthermore, it is quite ironic that Mephibosheth's city of refuge is called Lo-debar (2 Samuel 9:5). In Hebrew, this name conveys the idea of "no word". In other words, here was a man who was a crippled, living in the land of silence. In addition, he was a character whose name was rooted in "shame" – from the Hebrew word *bosheth*.

It never ceases to amaze me that when the mirror of our own life is held up before us, we are always brought face to face with our past. The narrative of the life of Mephibosheth would be a constant reminder of my former, silent and shameful condition. And I, not unlike Mephibosheth, but for different reasons of course, could not look the King in the eye. Yet, I also remember that it was the King – namely Jesus – who would personally escort both Mephibosheth and me to eat at His table. For both of us, love was unleashed and a destiny was changed. When all else is falling around us, love is the one constant which remains. However, in order for me to arrive at that place, a huge amount of work had to transpire before that script could ever become a reality.

The enormity of the challenge which lay before me related very much to the discovery of God's "deeper magic", made powerfully incarnate in the person of Jesus the Nazarene. This deeper magic could be epitomised by one word: love. This love actually drew my mother and father, my brothers and me into its strong current. They did not drown and neither did I. Each of us began to learn how to swim. We would go against the tide of what we had always known. We would learn to master strokes which would plunge us deeper into the ocean of God's unfathomable depths of love and grace. Each of us would undergo a radical transformation. This would be God's deeper magic at work in human lives.

Solvitus Ambulando cum Deo

The words *solvitus ambulando cum deo* translate as, "It is solved by walking with God". This Latin dictum would become the creed which would shape my spirituality over the coming days, weeks and months – in fact, right up to this present moment. The whole idea of God and religion in my world could be readily reduced to two specifics: one a tradition and the other a significant person.

In relation to the first, I keenly remember as a boy, our occasional attendance at the Greek Orthodox Church in our suburb. When it was Easter, our family would receive red Easter Eggs from relatives who devoutly attended. This was all part of the Greek Orthodox Church tradition. The eggs symbolised the celebration of Easter and the red, I had assumed, would have had some bearing on the death of Jesus, His blood being shed. The inference for my conclusion became increasingly obvious in later years.

The second specific, however, involved a person. It was no one who was close to me or my family. Neither was it someone whom I had looked up to as someone of significance or prominence. It was the old Anglican priest who taught the religious instruction class and had worked for many years in China. For me the ritual of religious instruction had always followed the same routine. My disruptive behaviour had always secured for me a prime position of being perched on the veranda outside the classroom. I had made up my mind that I was not there to learn and it was patently obvious that it would be more beneficial for the class that I was put out of the classroom.

Even though I had known that my behaviour was disruptive, nevertheless, I was always apprehensive about been outside. I was on the outside of the room but, my insides were like a churning sea. Primarily because I knew that the principal would often go on daily patrols. If ever a student were found by the principal, this would incur not only a serious discussion, but also disciplinary measures, which could potentially lead to suspension or even expulsion.

Nonetheless, my fears were allayed. The principal, for some

strange reason, never came and visited with me on the veranda.

Unbeknown to me, God's Deeper Magic was already at work with this Anglican priest. He would be the one who would lead me into the strange, unmapped, new land of God. This was all quite bizarre, considering the fact that this would all take place many years after I had left the school.

Upon leaving school, I developed a relationship with a man who was a ladies hairdresser. He too had had a terrible relationship of abuse with his father. We immediately hit it off and soon became the mournful duet, *You sigh for me and I will cry for you.*

I was soon well into my hairdressing career with my own business and a lifestyle with no moral compass, especially when it came to sexuality. Outwardly, I maintained a façade of having it all together. This was not too difficult, especially in my world of cosmetics and image making. Yet my resolve to *fake it till I make it* in my daily life became all the more complicated by what I now know as serious soul pain. No matter how much effort I invested with my brain and my body to resolve or attempt to anaesthetize my inner pain, the pain which enveloped me transcended the physical, the emotional and the intellectual. I could not extricate myself from it.

I remember a client in the hairdressing salon who had been studying Jungian Psychotherapy. She was elderly and her acumen had always greatly appealed to me. One day in the salon she passed a note to me. It was her interpretation of the writings of the Swiss psychiatrist, Carl Jung. Her scribbling on the note read...

"We can know with some degree of certainty that if we get rid of the pain before we have answered its questions, we are not only avoiding facing the terror of our pain, but also, we are actually getting rid of the true self whom we were meant to encounter."

Indeed, pain offers us questions to listen to. My dilemma was my sense of helplessness on two fronts. On the one hand, I knew that I was not able to provide adequate answers for the questions that the pain was demanding of me to answer. And on the other hand, I had too much pride to tell anyone about my private world. The bottom line was that I was plain scared. I did not want to be found. I was still hiding. That was the name of the game. I had become proficient in the art of disappearing.

My unrelenting soul pain drove me often to walk along the beaches of the Gold Coast of Queensland early in the morning, before the sun woke up. I would simply cry out to the darkness to hear me and give me the ability to live without such hatred and a deep dread of others. But my penchant towards death increased. The one word which resonated and throbbed within my head and heart was simply, *Why?*

What I have discovered over the years is that this conscious soul pain is true for all "sons of Adam and daughters of Eve".[3] We all protest what is happening within us. We all struggle in desperation while the waters swirl around our souls. Each of us is aware or becomes aware that even the very knowledge we possess appears impotent to prevent us from drowning. I had resolved, therefore, that it must be better to cry "Why?" than not cry at all. In hindsight, I realise that implicit in the question *why* is a belief that someone far bigger and greater than me exists who can hear and answer me. To not cry at all, allows despair to become absolute.

Alone and empty, the unimaginable occurred. A knock on my front door broke the early morning silence. It was the Anglican priest from my school days. He had come bearing gifts: a book in his hand and some words. He said to me that because he knew that I was into meditation and contemplation, he had brought me a book of Hebrew poems. It was the book of Psalms. He simply said that I might like to meditate on these verses. The other gift was expressed in seven simple words: "Van, I pray for you every day." Rather nervously, I became quite aware that his rather simple words touched something in me – or at least someone hiding deep down inside of me.

Could it be that what seems to be chaos is actually the birth of something new? I wondered.

His closing remarks were like a summoning imperative:

"If ever you want to come and walk with me around the island where my wife and I live, I will wait for you at 6.00am on the pier for the ferry to bring you from the mainland. Just let me know when."

As unassuming as his arrival was, so was his departure. He was gone with his mission accomplished. I certainly was not prepared for this unexpected intrusion.

Who could ever have thought that my inner world of rubble and ruin, which I could no longer control, was, paradoxically, the work of God – the best interior decorator going?

Hard drinking and further bouts of deep depression, however, began to take their toll on my life. My outrageous sexual escapades and alcohol abuse found me disillusioned and disenchanted with using others and being used also. Be it men or women, my proclivity to punish far exceeded the pleasure. Furthermore, I began to isolate myself and spend more time adjusting to the rhythm of withdrawal rather than frequenting familiar habitats – to the extent that even my early morning ritual of long walks and crying out to the darkness had abated considerably. On a daily basis I was able to maintain a certain degree of control in order to perform my tasks and maintain the business with the staff I had employed.

There were two more areas which had created great consternation in me. These were perhaps the most bizarre features of my world. I soon discovered that in the course of my conversations, I would begin referring to the contents of that Hebrew book of Psalms. Similarly, with recurring frequency, the words of the priest would cause a jabbing sensation in my memory regarding his invitation to come and visit with him. Eventually I capitulated. After all, *what on earth did I have to lose?* I had known for a long time that deep down the desperation which I had accommodated in my soul was larger than life itself.

I made arrangements to meet up with him. I arose early and headed off to the ferry. There in the distance across the waters, I could see a figure standing tall on the pier. His face lit up when he saw me. He greeted me warmly. We did not go into his home, we simply walked together. The entire walk around the island would take approximately thirty to forty-five minutes. He and his wife had worked with the China Inland Mission for many years. His wife's lineage could be directly related to Susannah Wesley.

My first walk with him left me in no doubt that it was a totally unappealing experience! I was not sure whether I would ever want to return to spend time with this man again. The thought undergirding my rationale was that he never asked me anything. Neither did he respond to the questions I threw out to him. If first impressions were meant to be lasting impressions, I was clearly unimpressed. Honestly, I found him to be the most uncaring and unloving human being I had ever been with!

In my secret yearnings and in my grinding despair, he offered me absolutely nothing. To further compound my reaction, upon leaving to embark on the ferry he invited me to return for another visit and a walk. I thought to myself, "This old man has testicular fortitude!" My thoughts concerning the walk with him were as unrelenting as the waves before me...

- Was he so oblivious to me?
- Was he so full of himself that he couldn't really see me?
- Would my existence be forever defined by a closed sky?

Over the waves back to the mainland and with the long drive home, I was aptly afforded the luxury of time for reflection. My imagination had not been gripped by some burning insight conveyed by him in our walk to convince me that he had anything to offer. But as I looked out on the broad expanse of water before me, I was made acutely aware that whilst I appreciated the surface of the shimmering blue waves, I had absolutely no idea what was going on in the depths of the ocean.

In my moment of philosophical reflection, little did I realise, God's Deeper Magic was working its way into my life. What I looked like on the surface to many had no consistency with what was true in the depths of my broken soul. There was a jarring dissonance. And then it was like an epiphany. I saw him. The presence of the priest was larger than my fear, larger than my anxiety, larger than the *seething dishonour* – like the old threats lingering unresolved from my childhood. The epiphany punctured my worldview.

The priest, he came with outstretched ears. He came with his ears bent close to my lips.

Throughout that island walk he was the first person in my life who had simply listened to me. He heard me. He did not come armed with an arsenal of good counselling techniques. He did not come ready to meet my expectations. He was there, fully present to me, with me and for me.

In my narcissism, in my recalcitrance, in my loathing self-indulgence, could it actually be that my ears were inattentive, waxed and uncircumcised?

Before the day was out I had determined that I would make contact with the priest and meet up with him again. And, of course, true to human form my good intentions remained just that: *good intentions*. The weeks passed and I had not made good on my intention to visit and walk around the island. The weeks turned into months and despair once again caught me in its tentacles. My brooding disposition and my attempt to masquerade as a lively and animated person was my demise. I could not sustain such a farce.

I began to grow deeply aware that I had to face my own impotence. I felt that I had to let go of the images, both positive and negative, that I had constructed and become so obsessively attached to. The Orthodox theologian Alexander Schmemman saw into the human heart when he made the following observation:

"It is not the immorality of the crimes of man that reveal him as a fallen being; it is his positive ideal – religious or secular – and his satisfaction with this ideal."[4]

A further three visits to the island eventually came – each characterised by the awkward rhythm of his deafening silence and my determined speech. He remained true and consistent to his person. All the while the incessant question remained in my heart and mind: *Why was it that I felt so disingenuous and hollow beside this old man?*

The battle is lost or won in the secret places of the will before God, never first in the external world[5]

Just as the priest had arrived at my door so unexpectedly many months before, so he came again without notice, bearing a gift.

He drew out of his bag another small book. He told me that this was a story of a man I must meet. I was more than intrigued by how emphatic he was, especially knowing that this priest was a man of very few words. He left me alone with the gospel of John. As soon as I had opened the first page, I found myself transfixed on the fifth verse of the first chapter:

"The light is shining in the darkness and the darkness could not extinguish it."[6]

This particular verse remained obstinate and punishing. It halted me in my attempt to push further forward in the text, in order to encounter the man who I must meet. Even when I ventured on in my reading of the first chapter, my mind would be drawn inexorably back to that fifth verse. My only option was to get on with my day and think that perhaps later I would return to where I first began. But I was astonished that throughout that day and the coming days, both my mind and my heart felt like they were impaled on this text. It transcended the very print on the page; it was living and breathing inside of me and demanded something from me. What that was remained elusive and enigmatic. The Anglican priest would be my only option and last resort.

It was July, late afternoon, early evening. I arrived home from work and settled down in my comfy old chair with a glass of red wine. I grabbed the small book, determined to treat it like any other book to read. Such bravado and boasting was soon reduced to a numbing sensation which I had never experienced before. I actually felt a growing awareness of thick darkness enveloping me all over. It soon became quite unbearable. In order to ease my discomfort, I managed to wriggle out of the chair. I found myself with my face on the floor. I had known what it was to be under the influence of a drug or alcohol. But this sensation caused such experiences to pale by comparison. My mouth became taut and

I was gasping for air. I soon discovered that I was unable to speak. I could not even open my mouth. The whole atmosphere was charged with prowling darkness.

The telephone rang, but I could not pick myself up off the floor, nor move towards the phone to answer it. My legs were like lead. In fact, my whole body was like lead. My external world and my internal world appeared to be contesting for something. The answering machine came on. The voice I heard was that of the Anglican priest. He simply said, "Van, it is going to be alright." I had absolutely no idea what he meant by those words. All I wanted to do was to drag myself off to lie in the bathtub. In the bathtub I felt that I had wanted to die.

Immediately, I began to experience the strange sensation of shards of light hitting my body. It was a very real physical sensation. Inwardly, I was conscious of the contest of my life. It was a life and death struggle. Previously I had made some rather vain and futile attempts at suicide, but this was entirely different. The very verse of scripture from the little book – *the light is shining in the darkness and the darkness could not extinguish it* – intensified its authority over me and within me. I had no speech to respond with, yet it was speaking to me; it was alive and potent; probing and wounding, prodding and unrelenting in its mission to secure a response from me. My world, the world within which I had never allowed anyone to enter or see, was not only engulfed in darkness, but the light was making its presence felt.

Similarly, the bathtub was not without its intruding images. The strongest memory which had surfaced related to Rhonda's dying and loss of blood in the bathtub. Admittedly, I had been conspicuously absent from being present to witness her bleeding and dying in the bathtub, yet, in my moment of flight from the bloody scene on that tragic day, my imagination had nursed a million and one scary scenarios. However, on this day, I felt that I was bleeding and dying.

Could this be my death? Was it really me who should have died on that cruel and tragic morning?

Gradually, I was being opened up by the scalpel of that ominous and unrelenting text from John 1:5. The light had exposed those inner recesses of my childhood memories. Darkness, on the other hand, was strangely peculiar and so unlike my many previous encounters. In the words of Paul Simon, it was for me the usual, *"Hello darkness my old friend, I have come to talk with you again..."* This time, however, its presence was so much more forceful, demanding and unfamiliar.

It seemed like a siren of voices screamed inside of me. What was so startling was that I had heard these voices many times before, yet now they were howling screams. One by one, the names of my imaginary childhood characters were mentioned, calling me to run to them. There they stood defiant and erect; all my imaginary friends – those whom I had welcomed so long ago and who inhabited my world of fantasy. It had been ages since I had last spoken to them or entertained their presence in my life. Each of their familiar faces melted before my eyes. It was like they had been wearing masks all along. Behind their masks were faces so hideous and grotesque that I was terrified. Their threats did not wane. The dangers were not imagined. Nothing could siphon off the uncontainable fear which had manacled me to their hold.

The dilemma was as large as Everest itself. To consent with my innermost being to the light would mean I had to face what I had hidden from for all the years of my existence. Conversely, to comply with the darkness would mean that I could go on mastering the art of disappearing: using and abusing, manipulating and contriving façades and foils in order to commodify people as mere things, which existed solely for my punitive agenda and pleasure. It seemed that from nowhere my dilemma had been interrupted by a chorus of voices. Each voice made its presence known in that bathtub ordeal. The first was the prophet Kahlil Gibran. His words came to me as if they had been shot out of a cannon into my soul...

"Your pain is the breaking of the shell that encloses your understanding. Even as the stone of fruit must break, that its heart may stand in the sun, so you must know pain. Much of your pain is self chosen."[7]

The second chorus, if that were not enough, was from Dylan Thomas the Welsh poet. He conspired to speak as well: "Do not go gently into that good night." "Rage," he said, "rage against the dying of the light."[8] For goodness sake, rage was all that I had known.

How was rage going to win this battle?

What was that good night which was beckoning me onward?

And so it began. Yes, I had wanted to die and die alone in that bathtub. And die I did. I gave in to the light.

I slept from early evening to very early the next morning. When I awoke, four things occurred. The first was that I devoured that little book, without any conscious recourse to the verse that had confronted and compelled me to surrender to it. The second was that the ominous presence of each of those fantasy characters which had been spawned in the cauldron of darkness was no more. The third, my bathtub became the place of nakedness, of openness, that bathtubs were designed to be. And fourthly, I met the man who I had to meet. He was on every page of that little book which the Anglican priest had given to me. His name was Jesus. Now I knew why He was so emphatic about meeting this man.

In that extremely vulnerable moment, I was given new eyes. The priest had prayed for me, just as he said he had, long after I had left school. And he had continued to do so right up to this very moment. I had felt so helpless and yet so helped. I felt so clean and unafraid of myself. Self-contempt had been transformed into compassion. The priest's seven words on my answering machine, "Van, it is going to be alright," were profoundly prophetic. Later, I would learn of Isaiah's words, *"Even before you called, I will answer..."* (Isaiah 65:24) and these conjoined with the priest's words were like good seed. Again, the Hebrew prophet Isaiah affirmed the reality of what I was beginning to learn:

"Just as the rain and the snow descend from the skies
And don't go back until they've watered the earth,
Doing their work of making things grow and blossom,
Producing seed for farmers and food for the hungry,
So will the words that come out of My mouth
Not come back empty handed.
They'll do the work I sent them to do,
They'll complete the assignment I gave them." (Isaiah 55:10-11 The Message)

Even though the bathtub ordeal produced no confession of the sinner's prayer in terms of faith for salvation, this act would come sometime later. I would find myself in the glorious company of the thousands of penitent seekers who had, over the centuries, responded to the invitation to become a follower of Jesus Christ. A dear friend, who stayed the long haul in my journey, had been able to help me to move on from my journey of self-effort to a new place of consciously surrendering my will to Jesus Christ as Lord and God. I emerged from the precincts of desolation into the new realm of desperation for God.

As for the Anglican priest, I so much wanted to rush to his side and walk with him. Intoxicated with such a sense of exhilaration, without any dependence on any substance, my eyes were wide open and alert to a strange, unmapped new land: the world of God.

What I had understood as serious soul pain had lessened immensely. Weeks passed and I decided to ring through to the cottage on the island where the priest lived. His wife answered the phone. She informed me that her husband had suffered a stroke and was paralysed. My walk with the priest was not to be. He could no longer walk and his speech was very slurred. I was now so ready to walk and learn from him the art of listening. I stammered and stuttered; I so wanted to pass on to him my seven words: "Robert, it is going to be alright."

I visited with him and our eyes made contact. He did not merely look into my eyes, however – he saw through them to my soul. He knew immediately, even before I could articulate it, that I had come to know the man Jesus. The burden he had carried had been rewarded. My opening words to him were simply, "Jesus was worth waiting for." But the more I had pondered that moment, the more I began to realise that perhaps it was the other way around: *Jesus had always been waiting for me.*

With shocking significance I had realised also that the priest had given me space to breathe. He did not set rigid entrance requirements. Somehow he knew me better than I had known myself. He was always so tight lipped. Even though he knew that prayer does not always give immediate feedback, he prayed. That night in July was not about me responding to his phone call. I had to *rage against the dying of the light* lest I miss *that good night* which was mine to embrace as a gift. The priest had seen and known *that good night* and he had been all the more tenacious in not letting go of God or me.

Could it be that he loved me, really loved me?

Deep down my world had been completely phony. My pretend world of euphemisms lay exposed. I had aligned myself with those who had cynically acknowledged none but themselves. Moreover, my fearful need to distort truth for the serving of my own self-interest was collapsing all around me. It was happening from the inside out. Yet somehow, I was overtaken with a fresh infusion of courage. For what, I was not so certain. Certain or not, I realised that the foreboding darkness was as light about me. That which threatened to overwhelm me was snuffed out by the inextinguishable blaze of light that drew me and awed me into arms that held me like a little child, helpless, defenceless and vulnerable.

Is this what John meant by "being born from above" or "born again" in his gospel?[9]

Whatever denominational religious category I had fitted into, after the rage sweetness had filled my mouth. I, who had been bewitched and so settled and at ease in false places, found myself in a new found land with explorer eyes, ready to move into dangerous places of newness where I would fear to go.

Guess who's coming to dinner?

My days as a hairdresser were becoming noticeably challenging. This became more obviously apparent as my hunger grew in the meditation of the Scriptures. My appetite was insatiable and prayer was a constant. My vocational life began to unravel. This was brought about through working my way through the Bible. It was the book of Ecclesiastes that really got my attention. The recurring refrain throughout the chapters – all is vanity – caused me to become more and more unsettled as a ladies' hairdresser. I finally conceded. Just as I had experienced those persistent, yet haunting words from the gospel of John – *"the light shining in the darkness and the darkness could not extinguish it"* – so too the phrase "all is vanity" was making severe inroads into my mind and my heart. I felt like I wanted to commit career-icide! The momentum was unrelenting...

- Was this actually God speaking to me?
- Was God attempting to get my attention?
- Was God really interested in me having a career change?
- What would I do?

Within months I gave up my job as a hairdresser and within a matter of days I had found myself going to work with my brother. He had returned to Brisbane from Sydney where he had been working. When he had heard that I had left my hairdressing career, he immediately said to me, "Would you like to have a go at being a brickie's labourer?" Admittedly, going from lifting hair rollers to carrying bricks was somewhat of a contrast, and the building site was a world away from the environment of a hair salon with its cosmetics and fashion magazines. Nevertheless, ready for the big day ahead of me, I started nice and early.

My brother had returned home to live with my mother and father. Nothing much had changed with my parents, if anything. My father was more subdued and my mother bravely clung to each new day. Mum was never the same since the death of Rhonda. The toll of incarceration and prison life compounded by her sense of estrangement from relatives and family, meant she had her own inner world of sadness and grief which constantly tormented her.

She had mountains to contend with. She was a deeply troubled person. The magnitude of her torment was unimaginable.

How could anyone ever truly live again after witnessing the death of their very own daughter through a flight of rage and a sharp knife by their very own hand?

Still, my anger towards both parents was seemingly unshakeable. Unforgiveness had kept the fires of anger burning. Oh, yes, I had been forgiven by God, but no, I had not forgiven my parents. This would be a long and torturous journey.

Meanwhile my adventures as a brickie's labourer could fill enough scripts to make a worthwhile comedy. The men on the job would routinely say, "Watch out for him, he used to be a ladies hairdresser … Don't turn your back on him…" etc. At the end of each week, before the working crew headed off to the local pub, it was a regular routine for them to dunk me in the water trough. It was their way of paying me out, their mode of baptism. It was also God's way of helping me to not take things so personally. This world was so different to the familiar, sanitised, perfumed salon of image-making and coiffures, which would dazzle even the conservatives among us.

Another feature of this new world that I had ventured into was their language. Colourful is a mild way of describing some of the banter that would go on throughout the day, not to mention during the lunch breaks. I decided that I would give them each a dictionary for a Christmas present to help each of them with their language. They were certainly not offended by this. If anything they were quite amused, considering the fact that the bulk of their conversations were largely monosyllabic!

What with regular baptisms, the gift of pocket dictionaries and also eventually being invited to comment on their so-called "friend's problems", this afforded me not only a sense of a place among them, but also the growing challenge to pray for them. Praying for them had a great effect on me.

I began to like these guys in a way that I could never have imagined. This was so very different to the way that I had looked at men previously. I saw them with new eyes and I prayed for them with a new heart. In addition, I began to feel more at ease with myself around them. My rationale for this sense of ease was that I was talking to God about them and God was talking back to me about them as well. He knew them better than I ever could or would. Just like the old Anglican priest, it was now my turn to take up the responsibility of prayer.

> So we bid You, by the time the sun goes down today
> Or by the time the sun comes up tomorrow,
> By night or by day,
> That you will speak in ways that we can hear
> Out beyond ourselves.
> It is Your speech to us that carries us where we have never been and
> it is Your speech to us that is our only hope[10]

It was Tuesday evening. My mother had invited me round for a meal. My brother was ever eager to boast to Mum about my crazy exploits in learning the life of a labourer on a building site. My mother laughed out loud. I had not heard her laugh for aeons. Her eyes lit up. She was almost unaware of anyone else around her. She looked so comfortable in her own skin. I must admit that I had not noticed this in her before, perhaps never. At the table my brother rolled out the stories of his younger brother attempting to navigate and manoeuvre a wheelbarrow filled with bricks across the uneven ground of the building site. I must have been such a sight to my workmates. He said that many had placed bets on me, as to whether I would actually make it to the other side with all the bricks in the barrow. More times than I could count those bricks would not all arrive at their intended destination. Not only would they manage to spill out, but I would also end up on my face in the dirt and mud when it rained.

Mum, my brother Ilo and me sat, ate and drank. I am not sure how it all happened, but there came a moment in the conversation where Ilo asked me: "So why did you get out of your hairdressing job to come to work like this and make a fool of yourself? Surely this is not where your future lies?"

I looked at them both and wondered what I would say. Then it came out like a torrent. There was no stopping me. "Since I have started reading the Bible," I began, "I am reading and hearing things that have made me think differently about the way that I have been living and the work I've been doing."

I must have mentioned the word "God" a hundred times. The name Jesus was certainly always in the forefront. The more I went on, the more animated I became and they became all the more engaged and intrigued. I can't remember how long I spoke for, but it was my first ever sermon – to an audience of two. That Tuesday evening we were all surprised that God came to the dinner table. My mother and Ilo gave their lives to God!

My brother had been involved in music, art and experimenting with drugs. I took him along to an inner city church. I had heard that this church specialised in working with men and women from this sort of background. He felt quite at home. They welcomed him with open arms. He immediately rang his girlfriend whom he had been living with in Sydney, and told her, "I've become a follower of Jesus. I'm singing songs about Jesus and I talk to Him and others about Him. I want you to come up to Brisbane and come to God."

She came and she did. Soon, they became involved in the life of that church community and they married. Years later, Ilo and his wife would leave Australia and live overseas. They are both currently involved in mission work with the poor in Albania. As if this were not significant enough, this church would also be the place where I would meet the woman to whom I am married to this day.

When Heazle first saw Ilo and I together, and because of my infrequent visits to the church, she said to me, "You are such a holy hermit. You have got to come down from the mountain and be with others." I resented her bluntness and did not appreciate this comment at all.

The truth of the matter is, that she got to me. Being a male, I was not going to admit that to her. My immediate stance was withdrawal – merely, of course, to lick my wounded pride. Even though I had God and the Scriptures, which I would devour, my brittle world, my inner world of fantasy was pierced through by her words. In fact, Heazle's words reinforced the truth that *human kind cannot bear very much reality*. I was unexpectedly uncovered.

More to the point, what she was saying would mean allowing another person into my life. I had absolutely convinced myself that I was really doing alright and holding myself together. Quite clearly, I was not ready for Heazle. I convinced myself that she would not be able to handle me. Pride again was decidedly waxing eloquent. How deceitful the human heart can be. Again I will reiterate what I have previously stated: *this would be a long and torturous journey.*

As for my mother, I had never attempted to venture into the wounded places of her heart. Mum and I were very much like two survivors. Our worlds had grown so far apart. Even though she was my mother, and we were both now following Jesus, discomfort and distance was evident between us both. Each of us knew that something was not right between us. Neither of us found it at all easy to speak of things past. There was an ominous sense of tiptoeing around on egg shells – each one of us precariously mastering the dance of avoidance and denial.

Our relationship was characterised by the awkwardness which people carry when they feel they don't know what to say. There is the awareness that something has transpired which has brought pain and loss, rupture and fracture to the relationship.

However, rather painfully, I realised that the greater loss is when we allow ourselves to be numbed by our own sense of impotence, when often all that is required is to simply be with the other person. Is that not what most people want anyway? Taken completely out of context, the words of David concerning our relationship with God and unequivocally with others had found their mark:

"Doing something for you, bringing something to you
that's not what You are after.
Being religious, acting pious
that's not what You are asking for.
You've opened my ears
so I can listen..." (Psalm 40:6-7 The Message)

Mum's employment and the conspicuous signs of her enjoyment in reading the Scriptures became the main topic of our conversation whenever we would catch up with each other. It was a new beginning for my mother. She would often ask me what I had been reading. I spent a lot of time in the Psalms. She too gained much comfort from them. Her growing hunger for the Bible caused my father to purchase a reading lamp for her. This way, she could read her Bible at night. My father was so much more subdued. His bouts of anger were much more infrequent.

Three months after she gave her life to God, my mother suffered a series of heart attacks. The doctor had said that she had carried some huge burdens all her life. They were all just too much for her to carry any longer. I knelt beside her bed. She was still alive, but she lay dying. She could not communicate. I held her hand. I was so sorry that I had not reached out to her and found those places in her heart. I cried and cried. In my desperation, I encountered my own sense of utter helplessness. I prayed and prayed to the God who we both were beginning to know.

My mother died at the age of forty-seven. The doctor simply said, "Your mother really died of a broken heart. She had never recovered from the death of her daughter, Rhonda."

I had beaten myself up for days, weeks, if not months. How long had my mother beaten herself up? The questions kept tumbling over and over without any respite or answer. And my prayers were not answered. Why? She died. Deep down within my heart, I knew that if I resisted the thought of giving up speaking to the very One who gave me a voice to speak, I would be resigning myself to desolation, to the even darker world which I had fled from. I could not reach her wounds. Did I even try?

I soon discovered that pain and loss have their own way of cleansing our perceptions.

Consciously, I had to recall and remember the fact that God came to dinner that Tuesday night to be with all of us. He had been received openly and not reluctantly. Eyes had been opened and hearts had been healed for my brother and my mother. Now, she is more alive than ever before in the presence of the Wounded Healer, Jesus Christ the Lord.

Forgiving God

My exorbitant self-indulgence blinded me for most, if not all of my life, to the people closest to me. As with my earlier years, I was much more superficial than I was willing to admit. In other words, my meditation and reading of the Scriptures did not really have access to my heart. My acquisition of the knowledge of scriptures, my ability to quote the word of God, decidedly and wrongfully merely caused me to construct a foil, in order to steel me with an image of having it all together. I was saved, but certainly not any the more honest with God or with Heazle and my friends.

My pathological blindness to my mother's brokenness was made all the more apparent when I met with my father. He too had a broken heart. He was not able to make up with his wife for all those years of cruelty and abuse. He had never spoken of Rhonda's death. Indeed, his aloneness was well served by his profound sadness.

Just like my mother and me, there was neither fondness nor warmth between my father and me. We both knew it. Our worlds were so disconnected. Too much had occurred. Both my brothers were now living overseas. I had married Heazle and had now set my heart towards going interstate to study the Scriptures further and be trained in pastoral ministry. I was glad of the fact that I could go interstate. At least, I had assumed, I would not have to face my father.

What we may choose to believe that we can run away from, we will eventually run into further down the track – namely, ourselves.

I studied with diligence and fervour, gleaning and gaining insights from the Scriptures. My pride in my studies, especially in biblical languages, and my fixation about knowledge merely galvanized in me a dogmatism which would cause me to gain from fellow students the award of Pharisee of the Year. I could quote scriptures quite freely. I would gain attention and acclamation from peers for holding court on matters theological and biblical. However, what I was in public and who I was in private were two different persons.

I found that I could hide quite easily from others by being able to wax eloquent with Scripture and other matters pertaining to God. Please keep in mind, that even though I had given my life to God, I had a very long way to go to get beyond the identity of Mephibosheth. It would only be in retrospect that I would realise that much of that identity was inseparably related to my father's misery and shame. Therefore, if ever I were to be extricated from that identity, a day of reckoning was inevitable between my father and me; indeed, a day which would also bring some healthy closure to the art of disappearing.

How one even begins to prepare for such a day defies sheer logic and calculated rationalism. One might attempt to calculate and strategise an appropriate intervention to resolve such an impasse. However, the more I would replay this scenario over and over in my mind, the more disquiet I felt. In my church life as a pastor, I would preach, teach and counsel others what to do in their many awkward situations. Regarding myself, I came up empty.

Why is it that so often, our last resort is God?

In 1987, Heazle and I had just returned to our home in Brisbane from a conference in Canberra. It was the first time that the late John Wimber had visited Australia and conducted a conference. It was unforgettable. In the first session I encountered God. It literally felt like I had been set alight with boisterous and uncontrollable laughter. At the end of the first session I had to be carried out of the auditorium by two men. With Heazle at my side they escorted me back to where we were staying. As we waited for the elevator in the hotel, I was slumped over the arms of our escorts. When we got into the elevator, there was a man who was also waiting to get in and it was rather obvious that he had spent some considerable time at the bar of the hotel. Obviously somewhat inebriated he looked over at me, as if to say, "What, you too?"

Intoxicated, smashed, whatever the expression best suited, I was well and truly gone. Finally, we arrived at the room where we had been staying. The men took me into the bedroom. I was out to it. Eventually, I woke up and no explanation had been given as to what actually took place between me and God. I was such an inquisitive person, but I was left stranded, coming up with no answers as to what God was doing. It was like that delicious moment in the conversation between Jesus and Nicodemus regarding the ways of God:

"The wind blows where it pleases, and you hear its sound, but you don't know where it comes from or where it is going..." (John 3:8)

Nicodemus, make up your mind, "What do you want to be, a weather forecaster or a sailboard enthusiast?" We cannot predict nor work out how God will bring about His purposes. In the words of Eugene Ionescu, "over-explanation separates us from astonishment, which is the only gateway to the incomprehensible."[11]

God was impressing on me, *"Put the torn and patched up mast of your life before me and I will blow it in the direction for which I have purposed. Trust me."* This was to be a lesson in faith. It was one thing to teach it and quite another to live it. Moreover, faith is born in the unfamiliar, not in the familiar. The predictable and the routine is not where you will find faith. It was like God was impressing upon me,

"Allow yourself the luxury of letting me show you how much I cannot be 'worked out' by your best theological explanations or tried and tested, well-worn doctrines. I know what I am doing with you. I am not accountable to you. What I am about is what you need to be about. Be receptive and attentive to My voice. What I have purposed for you and your father is more My business than your business. Besides, if I told you, you would not be able to handle it anyway ... I am merely educating you into ignorance."

Coming to my senses – if that is what you can call it – in the hotel room, Heazle astutely commented, "Van, this was God's way of wanting you to experience what it means to laugh as a child without any inhibitions. This was for you."

This would be the very beginning of a long and winding road of healing and recovery. Strangely enough, the next day, a colleague in ministry saw me prior to entering the conference centre and enquired as to where I was going to sit. I advised him of the place. I asked him why he was interested. His response was: "I just didn't want to be seen with you. Yesterday, you were so totally embarrassing; you were off your face." It was precisely in that situation and the many more which would follow in my life, that God had two lessons in mind for me. The first lesson...

"Learn to listen to your wife. She knows you better than you know yourself. Do not be a fool and give into the judgments and perceptions of others who do not know you nor love you as much as we love you."

And the second lesson from theologian Leslie Zeigler:

"This God who tells Moses, 'I am Who I am', who enters into

contingent relationships with human beings at particular times and in particular places, who approves of certain actions and not of others, has always been, to say the least, hard to live with. Human beings have always preferred gods for whom they can write their own job descriptions themselves."[12]

Did I get the message? Yes and no. Yes, this would take a lifetime working it out, perhaps another book. And No, precisely because on the one hand I had assumed that I knew myself better than my wife knew me and on the other hand, my arrogance concerning God was distinctly odious. In other words, we think we know ourselves better than we think. Obstinacy and arrogance are merely the landmines within us that God is after. His desire is to transform them into transparency and humility, rather than allowing them to be destructive mechanisms detonated by our own stupidity to cause explosions among our relationships with others.

Having arrived home in Brisbane I had immediately wanted to ring my father. I called and enquired as to his health. He mentioned to me that he had recently had an eye operation and something was irritating his eye. He had not been back to the eye specialist. Heazle and I dropped in to see him. Sure enough his eye was quite red and swollen. Because we had just returned from the Healing Conference, I was very much a "victim of the last conference".

Immediately I said to him that Heazle and I had just come from a Healing Conference in Canberra and would he allow us to pray for him? He reminded me that he was not into that sort of stuff. Eventually, however, he conceded. The incident still plays out with such vividness as I am sharing it with you. We stood before my father and I placed my hand over his infected eye. We prayed and then I removed my hand from his face. I asked him, "Dad, did anything happen?" Keep in mind, this was a man who had not been able to resolve his guilt and shame regarding his wife and his reckless lifestyle and, not forgetting, the deep grief over the death of his daughter many years before. Plus, who knows what he felt regarding his own sons. His response was breathtaking:

"The moment you put your hand on my eye I felt heat flowing into it. It was like something was drawn out from the eye."

We set out for home and said goodbye to my father. I rang him every second day and enquired about his eye. He said, "When you come next Sunday, it's my birthday. Will you pray for my back? It is as sore as ever. My eye is much better."

Something was definitely on. Heazle and I and our children arrived at my father's home for his birthday. He was glad to see us all. His eye was definitely so much better. His focus was immediately on his back being prayed for. We stood before him, just like last time. I was a little to the side with my hand on his back. Heazle also stood behind him with her hand on his back. As I continued to touch his back I began to feel tears welling up in my eyes. I turned to Heazle and said could she take over for me. Again her words penetrated my flimsy armour. She replied, "Van, this is between you and your father."

She continued to pray silently. I took my hand away from my father's back and placed it on his heart and then the tears ran down my face. I looked into the eyes of my father and from my heart the following words flowed:

"Dad, you know how your eye got healed last Saturday? The God who healed your eye can also heal your back. But not only that. I also need to tell you that He sees your heart and He knows what you have kept hidden in it for a very long time. He can heal your heart as well."

Then the unthinkable occurred. I could not get my head around it. It did not come from me. It was totally not from any theological journal or text book I had studied. Tears were running down my face and the words came to me...

"Tell your Dad that it is OK to forgive Me. He wants to say to Me, 'I forgive You God.'"

Where on earth was that in the Scriptures I so loved? I relayed God's message to Dad and immediately he began to speak to God in his native tongue, Albanian. I knew very little. I had studied Hebrew and Greek — I was not at all familiar with Albanian. Both Heazle and I listened in amazement. Neither of us could comprehend what he had said to God. We both knew, however, that he had made some sort of connection. We know, when we hear someone speak or sing in another language, that we can still be moved in our souls. Heartfelt passion goes beyond the realm of mere intellectual comprehension. This was no different. We were being moved beyond our limited language into an arena that was sublimely divine.

Yes, my father had asked Jesus to forgive him and heal him. That Sunday, on his birthday, my father accepted Jesus as the Lord and Saviour of his life. The psalmist's words capture profoundly what had transpired on my dad's birthday:

"I will mention those who know Me: Rahab, Philistia, Tyre and Cush — each one was born there. And it will be said of Zion, 'This one was born in her.' The Most High Himself will establish her. When He registers the peoples, the Lord will record, 'This one was born there'." (Psalm 87:4-6)

The names which were recorded here were representative of the fierce enemies of the people of God. Nevertheless, astonishingly and amazingly their ominous and terrifying reputations would be no match for the incomparable power of the living God. Like my father, mother, sister and brother, their names would be recorded in the Book of Life. Over the coming weeks I would visit with my father and help him on his new journey in discovering God. Here I was, introducing my father to the heavenly Father, the perfect Father. Together we met and read and prayed.

However, rather sadly I need to express this – that even with the unmistakable artistry of God's healing of my father's eye, his sore back and his broken heart, my inner life was none the more tender or receptive to my father. Unforgiveness continued to cast its spell over me. Deep down, I knew that I wanted something from my father.

I was no different to the Hebrew prophet Jonah, who was resentful that God would even want to pour out His mercy and grace upon the wicked Ninevites. Similarly, I too had resigned myself to the fact that I was resentful that my own father could be healed by God. I waited with bated breath for signs of remorse from my father concerning the way he treated his wife, my mother and the rest of the family. I wanted my pound of flesh, not merely an apology. My own sense of grief, I now realise in retrospect, was well and truly related to my frozen anger.

I knew that I was in waters that were far deeper and swollen than I had ever found myself in before. Not drowning, yet immersed in depths unfathomable. My strokes to swim were ever so feeble. It was like being caught in a rip. I must not panic, but simply allow the current or tide to continue to carry me in this undulating rhythm of losing myself. In many ways, what I was losing was very much related to the false self which I had sought to protect. A self sustained and nurtured by addictive drives which had contained me and confined me.

Could it be that we can give ourselves to God, never truly losing ourselves, and still find our true self?

When the words "I love you" really matter

Unfortunately, much of my study of God had made Him an object of mere knowledge, to be reduced to a doctrinal spreadsheet. Yet God refuses this all the time, because God is intensely personal. Discovering this truth cannot be reduced to bringing God under a microscope like some sort of laboratory experiment. God knows full well that life with Him is in the messy arena of relationship. This is His domain where He comes to us, up close and personal. Sadly and alarmingly, we the followers of Jesus can become quite skilful as rhetoricians – merely talking a lot and dispensing loads of information about God and His ways with very little evidence of transformation in our daily living. I realise that this is my projection, perhaps because it is where I lived for so long and where God has exposed me on numerous occasions as a pastor and as a person. But as the days rolled on, my times with my father became increasingly characterised by generous scoops of surprise.

The day began in the normal way and I was on my way to my father's for our usual time together. I decided that I would drop into the local bakery to pick up something for afternoon tea with my father. What a surprise I received when the lady behind the counter said to me, "You are not Mark Shore's boy are you? You look a lot like him." I was bowled over. I said, "How do you know my father?" She replied, "Your Dad was baptised in our church last Sunday evening." I walked out of that bakery angry and adamant that I had been let down and disappointed.

Why would such a significant event be kept from me? After all, I was the one who led him to Jesus!

With clenched fists raised heavenward, I was resolute that God must speak to me. Sure enough, God was immediately on my case.

"You brought your father to Me and now I am carrying him. It is time to let him go. It is time for you to know that I am responsible for him and not you. You are to be responsible to him. The way you live and the way you love him is all that I am after between you and your father. I am quite able to handle everything there is about your Dad. Give him to Me."

What proceeded next was disastrous. Turning on God, I shouted, "I wanted to be there for my father!" It did not take very long for God to respond:

"No Van, you wanted to be there for you. You wanted to be seen to be the one who rescued him. You wanted to be the one who would be given the accolades for what you did for your father. Your disappointment is because you did not have any say in the matter. My gift is for you to know that your father has always been loved by Me. He just never knew how much I loved him. Now he does."

Petulant and pouting, I walked off shrugging my shoulders. Yes, I knew God was right, but I could not accept His wisdom. I proceeded down the road to my father's house. He was waiting, sitting in his comfortable chair. I was not sure how I would approach him, considering all that had ensued between me and the bakery lady or me and God! I walked into the front sitting room and my father said that he had two things to share with me.

"First," he said, "I received news that I have pancreatic cancer. It is incurable. Second, I am reading this book called *The Blessing*. It talks about fathers blessing their sons. I have never done anything like that with you. So next time you come on over, I want to pray over you. Is that alright with you?"

What news was this? Which way would I go and what would I say to him? I made up my mind that I would celebrate his baptism with him. Besides, I really could not cope with what he had shared with me. His eyes softened. It was a first for me. He knew where I was at. He could see into my heart. We ate and drank together. Without sounding irreverent, it was very much like a Holy Communion but with a Danish pastry and Lipton tea. He was not morose.

He was young in God and new at this journey of faith. It became increasingly evident that his faith was not wobbly, nor weighed down by the future foreboding of death having the last say. I was a pastor and teacher, trained and ordained; I had much to learn from my father. This rite of passage was truly God-given for both my father and me. As the days lengthened, Dad's illness took its toll. Quite keenly, I remembered watching my own children with my father in their early years. They were so uncomfortable around him. They had witnessed his moods and his sullen temperament. It had been quite distressing for them. Children are a lot like wet cement: impressions form easily and can remain somewhat permanently etched into their minds. However, so much had changed since those days. Now that my father had placed himself under new management with God they, like me, began to see a very gentle soul with a tender heart. It was so utterly crazy for all of us.

Everything was so upside down for me. I had so convinced myself for the past weeks and months that I had been introducing my dad to our heavenly Father. It was completely the opposite. God, in fact, was allowing me to meet my father for the very first time. He knew what it would mean to me personally and especially for my family to meet my father. He was not lost; it was really me who had to be found – found and exposed to the truth which would set me free; free to finally love my father as God had always wanted for me and my dad. And just to see our children embracing my father and kissing him, wow!

The day came when my father wanted to pray for me. I arrived at the usual hour. He was sitting in his chair, growing progressively thinner day by day. His frame was lean, but his spirit was strong.

Was he going to ask me what I would like him to pray about? Did he need my advice on this matter?

Can you see who was the focus of those questions? Yes, you're right, it was me. I had not progressed very far at all. I could hear the song loud and clear, It's all about me.

My dad asked me to kneel before him with my head in his lap. He placed his hands on my shoulders. I so much wanted to help him with the prayer he was about to say – in his words, "speaking a blessing over me". He immediately started praying, just like his first prayer, in Albanian. He prayed for quite some time. During the prayer I felt his hands moving over my back, like he was massaging me. When he had finished and through my tears, I asked him why he had moved his hands over my back. His response surprised me: "I did not move my hands once!" Immediately I knew that this profound moment was God-given. The image depicted by Jeremiah the Hebrew prophet of God as a potter, sculpting clay, came home to me with strong conviction. It was none other than God sculpting and shaping me in the lap of my earthly father. Indeed it was His deeper magic at work.

Even though I did not understand what my Dad had said, I knew that in praying in his native tongue, he had said what needed to be said without my coaxing or tuition. He got it so right the first time when he spoke with God, why should this time be any different?

Besides, it was my father's idea anyway. Or better still, my father had heard the voice of God, his Father.

As the days and weeks went on my father was eventually taken to hospital. A few weeks before he passed away, he called me to his bedside. My heart was heavy. I knew right up to that very moment he had never said "sorry" about anything to me. My father asked me to come and lay my head on his chest. He began to stroke my hair. No further words were forthcoming. We were still, we were silent. God began to speak to me.

"Who made you judge of your father? I am his judge. I alone call him to account. Give up your internal tirade of demands. You must let him go. To truly let him go, you must love him for who he is and not for what you want him to be for you."

In my heart, I whispered. I sighed ever so deeply words which I never thought I would ever want to say to my father. However, before the words came out of my mouth, the silence was interrupted by my father's words: "I love you." It was all over. The war was ended. The shorelines were not streaked with blood and carnage. I cried. He was still and went to sleep. It would only be a matter of days before he died. He would be at home with his wife and daughter in the presence of the Wounded Healer, Jesus the Nazarene.

The God who comes to us, comes to both surprise and awaken us to the reality that once we begin the journey with Him we will never be able to return to the place where we first started. It will always look different and it will never be the same. *His Deeper Magic* releases us like prisoners upon a larger world.

It is my hope that my story so far has captured your attention and inspired you to pursue with even more determination your very human journey of faith in the God who is up close and personal with you. The following chapter confronts us with what I would suggest is the greatest challenge of all: *to just be ourselves.*

Endnotes:

1. Barney Hamady citing Richard Mouw 'Exploring Deeper Magic,' in Making Life Work: When Life is Working You or someone you love (Oklahoma: Tate Publishers and Enterprises, 2008) p241.

2. E. Peterson comments that this meaning may be conjectural. Refer to First and Second Samuel, (Louisville: Westminster John Knox Press,1999) p173.

3. This is one of C.S. Lewis' favourite expressions for human beings from his Chronicles of Narnia (1949-1954). It first occures in *The Lion, The Witch and The Wardrobe* (1950: MacMillian).

4. A. Schmemann, For the Life of the World (New York: St. Vladimir's Press, 1998) p100.

5. This is taken from Oswald Chambers My Utmost for His Highest (Great Britain: Hollen Street Press Ltd, Slough, Berks, 1975) 254

6. There are many and varied translations of the word meaning "overtook, comprehend or understand". Eugene Peterson offers the *"...darkness couldn't put it out"* (John 1:5 The Message).

7. Refer to Kahlil Gibran, The Prophet (London: William Heinemann: 1980) p61-62.

8. Dylan Thomas, Do Not Go Gently into That Good Night composed in 1951, is considered to be among the finest of his works. This was originally published in the journal Botteghe Oscure in 1952.

9. Refer to chapter 3 in the Gospel of John. It is the story of Jesus and Nicodemus.

10. Edwin Searcy, (ed.), Awed to Heaven, Rooted to Earth: Prayers of Walter Brueggemann (Minneapolis: Fortress Press, 2003) p56.

11. Eugene Ionesco Decouvertes (1969)

12. Leslie Zeigler, "Christianity or Feminism?' in W. Dembski and J. Richards (eds.), Unapologetic Apologetics: Meeting the Challenges of Theological Studies Downers Grove, Ill: InterVarsity, 2001) p181.

"You are blessed
when you are content with just who you are –
no more, no less.
That is the moment
you find yourselves
proud owners of everything
that can't be bought."
(Matthew 5:7, The Message)

3
The Greatest Challenge of All: Just be Yourself

How often in the course of your life have you heard the well-meaning and sincere words of family, friends and colleagues, "Just be yourself"? You are about to deliver a talk or, you find yourself in the invidious position of being asked to do something that on the one hand you really want to do, yet on the other, you are terrified and scared out of your brain about.

What is it about this expression "just be yourself" that engenders such an array of emotional chaos and intellectual confusion?

Perhaps it might be because the person who we *think* we are may after all not be the person who God *knows* us to truly be? Before we scurry frantically for some answers in response to this dilemma, I would like to suggest that we return to the Garden of Eden.

It is always good to start at the beginning – and the very beginning of the human story with Adam and Eve may provide some pertinent insights into our dilemma.

We can only imagine that the Eden setting was the most idyllic scenario possible. Think about it: walking and talking with God the Creator and receiving first hand insight and inspiration, not only about who God is, but also about who we are in His eyes.

As breathtaking and amazing the Eden setting was, most of us who are familiar with the Adam and Eve narrative are also acutely aware that the idyllic soon became the tragic. Darkness enfolds the hearts and minds of Adam and Eve. They both embrace an insidious lie which sets them on a course of believing that they can find their true selves without any connection or reference to God.

The tragedy for Adam and Eve was that it would have serious implications. Not only would it create a huge distance between them and the God who loved to converse so freely with them in the Garden, but also it would take them both further away from the discovery of who they really were. Think of it: away from the very One whose eyes beheld them with unutterable love and unconditional acceptance. Therefore, we ought not to be at all surprised when it comes to the attempts of theologians and scholars to explain this tragedy; it has spawned a library.

The sons of Adam and the daughters of Eve have found that they are powerless to shake themselves free from the consequences of the lie which enslaved their first parents back in the Garden of Eden. These consequences had engendered the belief that they could actually discover who they really were without reference to God the Creator. To this day these consequences have continued to enslave all their descendants with a legacy of darkness, self destruction and ultimately death.

In addition, this lie not only produced alienation from God and one another, but also, disintegration within themselves – a disintegration so deep that it would cause every human being since those early days in Eden to be fragmented and not fully integrated and whole. As a result, every person carries within them an "intolerable burden of self-enclosure". This expression is an attempt to convey the idea of having immense difficulty, either consciously or unconsciously, of revealing more about yourself to others and especially, to God.

I referred briefly in my introduction to an incident that proved to be a truly defining moment in my life. It was of an overwhelming picture on the screen of my imagination of a great cathedral with a series of marble steps and the shattering of a statue on those steps which confronted me. These marble steps were bustling with people streaming in and out of the great cathedral and apparently for no rhyme or reason the tears flowed from my eyes. There was absolutely no explanation, that is, until I broke my silence.

This picture which God employed to confront me, caused me to be found. Quite literally, I felt as though I was brought out by the scruff of my neck, out that is from behind my walls of self-enclosure. Most definitely I was exposed and found wanting on two counts. I had clung to the lie that I had been a very open person and also, I had seriously thought that I had been a lover of truth. Little could I have imagined that the picture which God had used was neither intended to humiliate nor destroy me, but rather to humble and transform me. The work of transformation would move me from being a very self-enclosed person to one learning to become skilled in the art of not disappearing. In other words, it would set me on the path of learning how to celebrate the real wealth of self-disclosure, especially with God and with others.

I have no doubt that we can all agree that hindsight gleaned through reflection is always marvellous. Of course, there are certainly those Eureka, enlightenment moments which are definitely invaluable and life-changing when they occur. Yet, these are not standard fare and par for the course. I truly wish I could say to you that in accepting the picture with which God confronted me, that its transforming impact upon me was immediate and instantaneous. That was not the case at all. God had grabbed hold of me, while I had been reluctant and resistant. I fought with God and I would not give in, that is until Jesus' words made the decisive dent in my flimsy armour of self-enclosure:

"This is the crisis we're in: God's light streamed into the world, but men and women everywhere ran for the darkness. They went for the darkness because they were not really interested in pleasing God. Everyone who makes a practice of doing evil, addicted to denial and illusion, hates God's light and won't come near it, fearing a painful exposure." (John 3: 19-20 The Message)

If this had not been enough, the persistent voice of the Holy Spirit shook the very walls which I had constructed, so that I could no longer attempt to conceal my "...addiction to denial and illusion." Just as Jesus' words had made their mark, similarly, it had also been true of the psalmist David's words: *"What you're after is truth from the inside out"* (Psalm 51:6 The Message). My version of truth and God's version of truth were really not on the same page. Basically, what had to be done was for me to give up my pity party and surrender to Him. Even though I felt very wobbly and fragile, nonetheless, light had begun to penetrate my darkened conscience regarding the picture and the incident.

However, even with that growing sense of clarity, a question had assailed my conscience: *Why was I crying?* Through my tears, I could not believe how gut wrenching my pain had been. The only expression I could come up with was what I had previously been aware of throughout my early years, namely, *serious soul pain.* And the only recourse of action to escape this serious soul pain was always to pursue some serious head space. I consciously had begun to shift gears. I figured that by resorting to using my intellect, I could essentially avoid my emotional pain and thereby console myself. It was effortless to perpetuate this pattern as I had always manoeuvred myself out of facing my own crap. Indeed, I had welcomed my efforts with a note of self-congratulation. Yet, the more I had limped along in the corridor of my soul, the less I had been consoled. I soon became increasingly aware that the emotion which had wreaked such soul pain was none other than anger.

Worst of all, I could not reconcile how willing a party I had become to allow so much anger to be at home within me. My first priority had been simply holding myself together. Secondly, I had to locate where the focus of my anger had been directed. Repeatedly, I would say to myself, "I just don't know any more." Regrettably however, the impending choice I faced offered me no respite. To be honest with myself, let alone with God, would demand a mountainous effort.

Therefore, out of sheer desperation, I capitulated and made the admission to God that I knew what the statue represented. Undeniably, it was me. I was the shattered statue lying in a million pieces all over the marble steps and down onto the pavement. My conscience was ablaze with the growing awareness that God had wanted to shatter me for quite sometime. *Shattered into Submission* was the one headline seared on my conscience which I had not particularly wanted to see. In that act of submission before God, there was still more to emerge.

Even though shards of light had penetrated my darkened conscience, the same question persisted, *Why was I crying?* My inarticulate responses had soon welled up within me. My anger had found its focus. Like a switch set on "replay", the anger had been directed at the people who were coming and going in and out of the great cathedral. Over and over I saw familiar faces and yet no one even bothered to stop. No one had wanted to pick up the shattered pieces of the statue. I had served these people for so many years and I had poured out my life for them. I had invested so much in them, and now, no one, not even one person was interested in helping me.

Here I was, a teacher of the scriptures and a pastor. I certainly had known what it was to encourage people about being honest with God and also to challenge people to practice faith. From a theological perspective at least, I had convinced myself that my faith was intact. Yet astonishingly, God had not been my first resort. I actually recoiled at handing over my life to God. The whole survivor mentality ran much deeper than I had been willing to admit. I had not realized how deliberate I had been in creating such an array of coping mechanisms. So many people want to "get by" in life without ever really letting anyone get up close and personal. However, when it comes to God, He just loves getting up close and personal. When God is given the opportunity to move into our space, then it is that revelation is often forthcoming.

Now shattered and silenced, it was God's turn to speak. It was like I had been placed under vocal quarantine. If you had asked me which biblical character would have best represented me at this time, it would have to be Job of old. The opening words of chapter 38 aptly capture the spirit of this moment in my life. It felt like God's hand was over my mouth. In fact it was, because God wanted to speak.

"Yes you have been serving the people. Yet you have allowed

yourself to be made in the image of what the people wanted you to be for them. They have not stopped to pick up the pieces of the statue because I would not allow it. I have not permitted them to pick up the pieces. It would never have been enough to merely break you. This is my doing. This is why I have shattered you. The choice is before you: either you will place yourself in My scarred hands and allow Me to create the image of who you were meant to be for Me, or you will place yourself in the hands of people and so conform to the image of what they would have you be for them."

My brain was assaulted with a flurry of punches which came from every side and every angle. Each blow impressed upon me an array of questions:

- How do I respond to God?
- Do I go the way of God?
- Do I go the way of the people?
- What would I get out of this?

Undeniably, the obvious "I" in each question unashamedly made me the centre of the universe! Momentarily, I saw myself as a city in ruins. I took a quick glance around at the rubble in my life, but the sight was far too painful to linger there for very long. However, the choice was clearly placed before me. Like Job of old, I too had heard God's voice. It was the voice of the One who knew the worst about me and yet, loved me all the more.

Even though I had maintained my daily rituals of reading the Scriptures, regular prayer and serving God in the church, I had become quite skilful in my "addiction to denial". I believe that deep down, many of us may know this truth. If you do not think that this could be possible, think again. Let us eavesdrop on a conversation which Jesus had with some theological experts:

"You have your heads in your Bibles constantly because you think you'll find eternal life there. But you miss the forest for the trees. These scriptures are all about me! And here I am, standing right before you, and you aren't willing to receive from me the life you say you want." (John 5:39-40 The Message)

My moment had arrived. The choice had been made. I chose the way of the people. I placed myself in their hands. What had determined my choice was that I had believed I was in control of my life and my future. Having adopted this route with the people, I settled in for the long haul of putting myself together. I had lived a double life for a long time; this would be no different, really. However, even with the transaction done and dusted, I clearly wasn't prepared for what would unfold. Perhaps, at this specific time it would have been more appropriate for me to align myself with Humpty Dumpty.

From all sides, prominence and profile, significance and status came rushing in like a torrent. With both hands I awkwardly grabbed at everything which was coming my way. I did not want to miss out on anything. I knew that I was certainly not swimming very competently. If anything, it had felt like I was drowning and lost at sea. These powerful images of being lost at sea and clinging to the life raft of prominence and profile, significance and status, only reinforced my determination to keep God at arm's length. I once heard someone say something that has been indelibly engraved on my heart; something which I have not been able to forget: "Sin is instantly forgiven, but stupid is forever."

Strangely enough, however, it was precisely during these times that God was much nearer to me than I could even begin to comprehend or imagine. I was not unlike David who, out of the depths of his experiences with God, offered this precious insight: *"God is with me when I make my bed in hell"* (Psalm 139:8 The Message). And yet for me...

Why would I want to continue with the illusion that I could not be uncovered by God?

Especially when in Eden, God probed His rebellious child with the searching question, *"Adam, where are you?"* However, my stupidity continued. I maintained the belief that I could actually create invisible escape routes from the searching gaze of Him who sees all things. The wisdom of the following Hebrew Proverb apprehended me:

"Even hell holds no secrets from God; do you think he can't read human hearts?" (Proverbs 15:11 The Message)

Alone with myself and the choice I had made, I was on my knees. Something weird transpired. I experienced the sensation of droplets of water entering the pores of my soul. It felt as though the arid and parched places in my soul, which I had neglected in the busyness of maintaining my high walls of self-enclosure, were gradually moistened. Cracks began to appear. I was being opened up. Again, the psalmist David's words seeped through and began to nourish something deep within me:

"For day and night, your hand was heavy upon me; my strength was sapped, as in the heat of summer." (Psalm 32:4 The Message)

Paradoxically, I had been both disturbed by these words and yet, so irresistibly drawn to their reality: *"Your hand was heavy upon me."*

I had made the assumption that I could actually protect myself from God and from others. I had trapped myself in a prison of my own making – such had been the deceptive force of this intolerable burden of self-enclosure. It had caused me to think that I had been in control. This period, however, had been short lived. God began to make known to me that I was definitely not in control. All I had been in control of was my futile attempts at running my life, my way, without Him.

When we consider the portrayal of God's first encounter with humanity, it is one of Him taking a handful of dust and breathing into it. This is a profound picture of how utterly dependent we are on God the Creator. Life becomes more dust than reality when we pretend that we do not need Him. In Thomas Howard's exploration of T. S. Eliot's Four Quartets, Eliot brings the reader into "our first world", which is Eden, and after being drawn deeper into this mysterious place, a thrush tells us, go into the garden: "Go, go, go ... human kind cannot bear very much reality."[1]

I was simply like every other son of Adam and daughter of Eve, running away from God and re-enacting their rebellious dance in search of self-knowledge, but only on my terms. I had become skilful in two roles which were played out on a daily basis. I had not only become an artisan skilled at constructing walls, but also a prison warder. Day after day, I had been building walls for myself in order to keep others out and imprisoning myself in a world based on fantasy. Both roles had served to obstruct God and others from having access to me. Nevertheless, like the faint nuances felt in the early stirrings of the caterpillar breaking out of its cocoon, so too it was equally true of me. I was beginning to emerge from behind my walls of self-enclosure.

A caterpillar to a butterfly is certainly a profoundly beautiful transformation, but only for a few weeks – how much more a human being becoming who he/she is meant to be in the hands of the Creator? What would that human life look like for all eternity?

Remarkably, God was much more determined to reveal His love to me in order to overcome the estrangement between myself and Him; an estrangement brought about by my pride and rebellion. Because all humanity shares in the legacy of the lie bequeathed to them by Adam and Eve, all therefore suffer the same discontent. It is a discontent which impairs our ability to receive truth and also impedes our moving closer to the God who is truth. The very deception of self-enclosure reinforces a fixation towards self. This prevents us from seeing the truth that a person wrapped up in him or her self is a very small package; in fact, they have merely become a salesperson of their own ego. Self-enclosure also breeds an unhealthy preoccupation with self-importance.

Affirmation and admiration do have their proper place in our world of relationships, yet not when they keep us bound to,

"...addiction to denial and illusion, hating God's light and unwilling to come near it, fearing a painful exposure of who we really are" (John 3:19-20 The Message).

As a follower of Jesus, therefore, we must never to be taken by surprise when we discover that just below the shiny surface of our redeemed humanity we long for those five famous words: *"Everybody is looking for you"* (Mark 1:37 The Message).

If ever we are to grasp the skill involved in the art of not disappearing, we must be willing to relinquish any belief that breeds self-enclosure. Fundamental to the creed of self-enclosure is that it actually keeps God at arm's length. Not to mention, of course, what it does to those closest to us. What is even more astonishing is how long it takes us to comprehend that God cannot be kept at bay.

If there is a God in whose image we are made, then it would stand to reason that we would have a longing and a built-in craving for a life beyond all the restrictions of the horizons of this world. Could this be what is behind the idea that

"God has placed eternity in our hearts?" (Ecclesiastes 3:11 NIV)

In addition, this is equally true of any vocation which we foolishly believe could actually define our identity and destiny, worth or value.

Whether it was *Death at the Cathedral* or *The Day the Image Shattered*, I had gleaned some specific insights which have allowed me now to travel on the path of self-disclosure or become more skilled at the art of not disappearing. Yet, before we venture along that path, I want to qualify some of these specifics before they are offered to you. At all costs we must avoid turning every incident into a lesson from which we can extract some formula or principle. Not every experience we go through demands that we squeeze out of it some insight which will afford us with perspective and instant clarity.

The narrative of Job reminds us of this, in that God can do anything He wants without having to provide a reason (Job 2:3, 9:17). Sure, we may stop, analyse and dissect everything we can from our experience in order to download enough data to resource us for the journey ahead. However, the one constant remains: God is not accountable to anyone! God does not have to explain Himself. God does not live according to our script. When we do decide to move on in our journey with God, having exhausted all possible resources, then we must resolve either to remain impaled where we are or commence the steep learning curve of living with the unanswered. God, who is all wise, knows exactly when He will choose to dispense or withhold the wisdom necessary to give us insight into what went on in our previous experiences. Be absolutely assured that our apprehension of this insight will not be discovered merely by looking constantly over our shoulder.

Have you ever wondered why it is that when Jesus is teaching on faith or trust, He is not so much addressing unbelief, but rather, the eroding force of anxiety? [2]

Learning to live with the unanswered is much more about trusting God than we could possibly realise. Philip Yancey[3] sums it up so well: "Faith means believing in advance what will only make sense in reverse."

In the closing words of the final chapter of Job we are confronted with the probing insight of what our image of God is really like. We find Job at prayer. His insight draws our attention to a distinction which is clearly made:

"I know that you can do all things;
No plan of yours can be thwarted.
You asked, 'Who is this that obscures my counsel without knowledge?'
Surely I spoke of things I did not understand,
things too wonderful for me to know.
You said, 'Listen now and I will speak;
I will question you,
And you shall answer me.'
My ears had heard of you
But now my eyes have seen you.
In this I despise myself
and repent in dust and ashes." (Job 42:1-6)

This distinction is not merely and only between hearing and seeing; rather it is between knowing about something and knowing someone. It is between having a body of information and having an encounter with a person that is overwhelming and life-changing. From these closing lines in Job's narrative, self-disclosure comes at great cost. Job's defences have not only been shattered, but also his encounter with God did not bring the conclusion which one would surmise. It does not end with an expectant, jubilant hallelujah. In the words of Job chapter 42:

"My ears had heard of you
But now my eyes have seen you.
In this I despise myself
and repent in dust and ashes."

This paradox reveals that this shattering is essential for all of us. In our desire to know God, we must also be willing to be known by Him, but again, it must always be on his terms.

For me, without also paying the price, I would still be constructing higher and stronger walls and remain imprisoned to the scripts of my own fantasies and those of others. My experience has taught me that we expend a lot of energy in the creation of scripts of self-enclosure from an early age. In our early years we work hard at mastering the steps of the dance of denial. Rather tellingly, the Hebrew prophet Jeremiah suggests that there is an inseparable connection between denial and deception. This is so pervasive.

"The heart is deceitful above all things and beyond cure. Who can understand it?" (Jeremiah 17:9)

To see evil as parasitic is not to deny or trivialise it, but rather to see it for what it is. Other translations of the Hebrew text convey the idea of "desperately wicked, treacherous, perverse and devious..."[4] Therefore the addiction to denial is not such an awkward dance after all. Only too well do we know its incessant rhythm and yet, the Knower of hearts is none other than the Healer of hearts. With piercing perception the prophet grasped the revelation that all humanity requires radical, invasive, cardiac surgery. The prophet knew God and because of this knowledge, he could confidently assert, "I the Lord search the heart..." (Jeremiah 17:10). Yet Jeremiah does not leave us wondering what God will find and what God will surface. Rather with firm resolve, he cries,

"God pick up the pieces.
Put me back together again.
You are my praise." (Jeremiah 17:14 The Message)

In concluding this chapter and to lead us into the next, might I suggest that the following text directs you in your thinking and reflection in relation to what God has wanted to reveal to each of us from the very beginning of all beginnings:

"He [Jesus] *came to his own people, but they didn't want him. But whoever did want him, who believed he was who he claimed and would do what he said, He made to be their true selves, their child-of-God selves."* (John 1:11-12 The Message)

These words are from the Son who is the Knower and the Healer of all human hurts. God has always wanted us to be comfortable in our own skin, knowing that behind the eyes which see everything is a love that accepts and heals. Therefore, as we further explore this journey of self-disclosure with God and others, could it be that we will actually discover the truth that,

True self-denial is actually the way in which we make room for God in our lives.

The sooner we grasp this insight the sooner we will be empowered to receive all that God has and wants to give away to us. This will also have stunning implications in relation to a renewed appreciation of our humanity and a remarkable healing in all our relationships.

Foundational to this is that it all begins with the greatest exchange of all: our fallen selves for God's gift of our "true selves", our "child-of-God selves". From a Christian perspective, this understanding is often an overlooked feature of what salvation was intended to convey. This, among many other significant insights is precisely what the fourth chapter invites us to explore and examine.

Endnotes:

1. Refer to T. Howard, Dove Descending: A Journey into the T. S. Eliot's Four Quartets: Burnt Norton, Ignatius Press: 2006), p33.

2. In both the Hebrew tradition and the Christian tradition the theme is consistent; refer to Proverbs 3:5-6 and Matthew 6:25-34.

3. Yancey's informative insight is found in his book: Disappointment with God: three questions no one asks aloud (Grand Rapids: Zondervan, 1992), p224.

4. Refer to The Jerusalem Bible and The New Revised Version.

"Into that strange unmapped new land,
round the forbidden corner,
through the locked and bolted door
we grope

Prisoners released upon a larger world,
new freedoms frighten us.
We clutch old tasks,
familiar ways

Come now,
Lord of the old
and the new,
disclose to our explorer eyes
your new found land."
(N.T. Wright, Easter Oratorio)

4
The Greatest Command of All: Come, Follow Me

Often, in any introductory course in Theology, students would be introduced to the subject of The Attributes of God. During the course, they would explore fundamental aspects of His being such as His omnipotence, His omniscience or all-knowing-ness and His omnipresence. There is a fourth attribute to God's nature which I believe has a major bearing in understanding *the art of not disappearing*. Just as Moses in the desert stumbled upon the burning bush, so it was that I literally stumbled on this attribute of God while reading Mark's gospel:

"As Jesus walked beside the Sea of Galilee, he saw Simon and his brother Andrew net fishing. Fishing was their regular work. Jesus said to them, 'Come follow me, and I will make a new kind of fishermen out of you.'" (Mark 1:16-17 The Message)

These verses paved the way for my eyes being opened to this

fourth attribute. Namely, that Jesus is *Omni-Competent*. What I mean, is that *"*[Jesus] *can do anything ... far more than you could ever imagine or guess or request in your wildest dreams!"* (Ephesians 3:20 The Message)

In other words, all our brave attempts at making ourselves into what we may think will bring us significance or status, will pale in comparison with what takes place when we allow Jesus to be Omni-Competent in our lives. Recently, a friend reminded me that God saw me as play-dough rather than clay. Clay hardens, whereas, play-dough remains squishy and malleable. This is precisely what Jesus wants us to be in His scarred hands.

In my first year as a member of the faculty of a Bible College in Brisbane, Australia in 2002, I had been asked to teach The New Testament, New Testament Greek and Patterns of Spiritual Formation. Without in any way minimising the importance of the New Testament subjects, by its very name, Patterns of Spiritual Formation broadcasted loudly the given intention of the course. It was not that the other subjects were not of equal challenge. However, Patterns of Spiritual Formation would prove to be both *confrontational* and *transformational*, for not only the students, but also for myself.

In the previous chapter I referred to a defining moment in my life – the day the image shattered. It was this seed, sown in my life from that encounter with God, which would prove to be invaluable to this subject that I would teach. In relation to this subject, I enquired of God as to what He wanted to do with it. Eagerly and yet nervously, I waited with great expectation. Three letters began to form in my mind: VTR. Yes, that's it! VTR... Bear in mind that this was right at the beginning of the semester. Seeking a bit more information, I said to God, "You have got to be kidding? You gave Moses more than three letters. I've got to put together a course over 13 weeks of a semester. Would there be any chance you could do a bit better than three letters?"

Admittedly, it was a somewhat audacious response, yet I am sure of two things: God has heard it all before and, secondly, I'm sure you can identify with me. Unlike the woman who kept appealing to Jesus to attend to her severely demonised daughter and, *"Jesus did not answer her a word"* (Matthew 15:22-23 NIV), at least He had answered me. Then, just as the letters VTR gripped my attention, these three letters began to form into words:

- Vulnerability
- Transparency
- Responsibility

In that exchange with God, I was left with the clear impression that He was keen to use this particular unit as both the catalyst and the crucible in the formation of the students. This formation would not only be intellectual, but would also go far deeper into the interior of their lives, to the soul and the spirit. In Jungian psychology it would be classified as the ego – "the unobserved self". Most definitely it would be an interior work and who better to tutor me than the greatest interior decorator of all, Jesus Himself. The letters VTR were to become more than mere words. What developed was not merely and only a challenging subject for the students, it would also be my own obituary.

Vulnerability – meant no more WALLS – no more hiding; no more pretending

Transparency – meant no more MASKS – no more mere role playing; no more image-making in order to impress

Responsibility – meant no more EXCUSES – no more blaming everyone else; no more letting someone else pick up the tab!

My initial response to all three words was purely an etymological one. I could simply grab the Thesaurus and investigate the meaning of these words. As much as an investigation of the meaning of words can prove to be relatively helpful, it nonetheless has its limitations. For example, a mere cursory glance at the first word: vulnerability. In Latin *vulnerāre* conveys the idea "to wound". According to the Collins Concise Dictionary: the authority on current English[1], the word "vulnerable" means, "capable of being physically or emotionally wounded or hurt."

Now as much as we may not appreciate the following comments, and considering the daily grind of learning from life experiences, I have known and have experienced the reality of the voracious appetite of human beings, including myself, of wounding and hurting each other. Therefore, we ought not to be at all surprised that as people begin to grow older, they readily adopt an invulnerable posture. Rather ironically, Madeleine L'Engle[2] offers the following observation:

"When we were children, we used to think that when we grew up we would no longer need to be vulnerable. But to grow up is to accept vulnerability … To be alive is to be vulnerable."

On the other hand, when it comes to God, He is so wise. He has His own way of dismantling our preconceptions. God is wholeheartedly committed that we learn well. God knows that when we learn well we shall also live well. Yet even with my brazen efforts to bolster my own ego with the study of the origin of words, all the same I could not outwit God. On every count I continued to be completely outmatched. Gamesmanship from my perspective, though sophisticated, was entirely unconvincing.

And so it was that God's Spirit decisively manoeuvred some rather awkward words from Jesus into my space. It was these words which well and truly put me on the mat:

"A new commandment I give you; that you love one another. As I have loved you, so you must love one another. By this all will know that you are my disciples, if you love one another." (John 13:34-35)

Menacingly, questions arose:

• I had memorised these words. I had even taught from these verses. I loved speaking about these words. Why, suddenly, had these words felt so awkward?
• Was it that Jesus mentioned "love one another" twice in the first verse?
• Was it more related to the sobering fact that I had come up so short in the love stakes?

The awkwardness of Jesus' words ransacked me well and truly. I had readily identified myself with the prophet Isaiah's words, *"I am undone"* (Isaiah 6:5). It is one thing to believe that you are a warm, loving human being, and quite another to discover just how shallow that loving really is. And yet, when revelation breaks into our lives it is not always intended to leave us lying flat on our faces. Rather, the point about revelation is that what it illuminates is not always about what we have been unable to see. Often it is more about what we already see, but with the specific twist of actually knowing it for the first time. Nobel Prize winner T.S. Eliot reminds us that,

"We shall not cease from exploration. And the end of all our exploring will be to arrive where we started and know the place for the first time."[3]

Revelation is primarily God's initiative. He is intent on making Himself known to us much more than we want to be known by Him. Two elements of truth which God had revealed to me became increasingly apparent. The first one related to the fact that there could be no escaping from the inseparable connection between Jesus' new command of "Love one another" and those three words: *vulnerability, transparency* and *responsibility*. This new commandment could only find its true expression in and through people who were willing to become vulnerable, transparent and responsible. In other words, people who would be willing:

- to be wounded
- to be radically honest, and
- to be responsible

Outrageous admittedly, and yet the starting point is precisely when the sons of Adam and daughters of Eve give up their fallen selves to Jesus. The reason for this act of surrender is because our fallen selves are impotent to empower us to love in the way that Jesus challenges us to love. Every attempt to love out of our fallen selves will always have an inverted focus of me as the centre of attention. Such is the legacy of what we inherited from Adam and Eve. It had decisively brought about this inversion. This legacy of *inversion* necessitates conversion at the deepest level of the human heart – a conversion which can make vulnerability, transparency and responsibility a reality.

The second element which made the new commandment doubly awkward was the Greek word which Jesus used for "love" it was *agape*. The following bullet points do not even begin to fathom or touch the reality of the potency of this love. Nonetheless, we need to plunge ourselves into this melting pot...

- This love resists mere rational explanation
- This love goes beyond linguistic analysis
- This love is never neat and tidy
- This love is neither sterile nor domesticated
- This love does not manipulate or violate another
- This love is never about self-interest and possessiveness
- This love is sourced in God, for He is love

Immediately, my mind remonstrated: this love – *agape* – is totally impossible. Of course it is. As much as protest may have been the order of the day, yet astonishingly within the world of the New Testament, those who have surrendered their fallen selves to Jesus are soon made aware that, "God has not skimped at all in His generous gift of love."[4] Please let us get something straight here – the truth for me personally: I would have actually been exceedingly happier if the "new commandment" which Jesus gave in John 13:34 was, "that you understand one another." And why not, because it would be so much easier to rationalize, explain and fix up everyone. However, this was not what Jesus was after from His followers. He had simply and yet profoundly said, *"love"*.

It was like God was saying to me, "Stop asking the 'how' questions," because the "how" questions are very much focused on fixing everything and making sure everything is functioning properly. Fixing up everyone merely places "me" as the major player in the spotlight on centre stage, rather than the One to whom it really belongs, namely, God. How very applicable, therefore, are the words of Dostoyevsky: "If everything on earth were rational nothing would ever happen."[5]

How often I had heard myself saying, "Jesus, just give me

the tools and I can get on with the job, thank you very much."
His response remains consistently consistent and perpetually
permanent: "Love!" This *agape* love was intended to transcend
the rational. It is precisely when we are willing to take the risk of
loving, that we actually make space for God to move powerfully
through love. It is simply getting out of God's way so that God
can get on with what He does best: *loving people into wholeness
and giving them back their true selves.* Therefore, whenever love
is given away without expectation of reward, it makes the giver
all the richer, and all the wiser; when such love is willing to be
wounded, its wounds have the capacity to make a person all the
more whole.

Miracle of miracles, when love finds a home in the human heart,
that person is actually empowered to live as God had always
intended:

- Without secrets
- Without shame
- Without surrendering to any status symbols which merely
stroke the fallen self

*Rather surprisingly, the most startling fact about this love is that It
is a gift to be embraced; it can never be earned, nor can it ever be
received on the basis of being good enough or worthy enough. It
must be given before it can be returned.*

Think about the way that God sees people: we were His by value
of creation, made by Him and for Him. And secondly, we are His
again by the value of redemption, freed from our fallen selves and
now, freed into being our true child of God selves! And this is all
because of Jesus' death and resurrection.

Every son of Adam and daughter of Eve who has surrendered

to this furious, irrational love of God, namely, Jesus, now find themselves catapulted into the brave new world of loving without expectation of reward. We soon discover that the success of love is in the loving, not in the result of loving. What can often be overlooked is that this love is not to be viewed as mere virtue – as if it is something which we can manufacture or reproduce with sheer will and determination. Dante reminds us that, "Love is the energy that moves the sun, the moon and the other stars."[6] In light of Dante's eloquent observation, what needs to be grasped is that this amazing *agape* love actually carries within it all the powerful ingredients to energise and empower us to truly live and experience ever-increasing wholeness, dignity and freedom. Therefore we can never be and will never be the same, ever again.

Sure, we can return to where we came from. And yet, it will always be with very sad consequences. Everything about where we came from and who we have attempted to be is brought into sharper relief.

Think about it: if Adam and Eve really were secure in who they were in God's love, they would not have been seduced by any other rival.

Life outside of Jesus is nothing other than mere enslavement to self and it is detrimental and toxic. Self-love is so horribly touchy.

This is precisely why Jesus had to come for us. Loving ourselves the way in which Jesus is calling us to love is always about honouring and respecting ourselves and others enough to not go on playing out the patterns of denial, deception and destruction in all their tragic forms. The world's way of love is that love is a trick to make a person vulnerable in the most deceptive and tragic sense. People are then depersonalised, dehumanised and therefore used as mere commodities. I had done this for years.

God wants us not merely to grow old, but also to grow up, fully alive to His love and responsible as lovers of His Son.

"He [Jesus] came to his own people, but they didn't want him. But whoever did want him, who believed he was who he claimed and would do what he said, He made to be their true selves, their child-of-God selves." (John 1:11-12 The Message)

Did you know that God always wanted to give you back your true self?

This was never an afterthought or Plan B because Plan A had failed so miserably on the part of God the Creator. This language of true selves may appear to be clumsy and difficult to grasp. Primarily, it is because we cannot grasp just how much we camouflage ourselves with roles, successes and satisfying explanations as to who we think we are. People spend such an excessive amount of time and energy in the pursuit of what they think will give them significance, success and security. Yet worst of all, often it is without any reference to God at all. Jesus unmasks this pervasive deception:

"What good would it do, to get everything you want and lose you, the real you? What could you ever trade your soul for?" (Mark 8:37-38 The Message)

Therefore, if ever we are to grasp some sense of what this expression true selves means, we need to return again to where it all began. Basic to biblical religion is that we were made *"in the image of God"* (Genesis 1:26). Basic to this truth is that God wants every human being to know that they already have inherent, inborn value and intrinsic worth.

When Adam and Eve turned away from God in order to become

what they wanted to be on their own terms, they deceived themselves. They had exchanged true worth for an illusion of what value and worth was, according to their script. Worst of all, their capacity to become vulnerable, transparent and responsible human beings, even in a very nascent sense, was lost. It was such a high price to pay. *Intimacy and self-disclosure with God had been exchanged for isolation and self-enclosure.* The magnitude of their alienation escalated to the extent that they had become entrenched in the lie that they could live without the One who had given them true value and worth.

Having said this, one cannot ever be dismissive of the fact that the father of lies[7] was at work. He was there in the beginning and, of course, now at work in the world. His prime strategy is not merely to discourage, but chiefly to keep people from thinking about God. This has major bearing on the person of Jesus. The "father of lies" knows full well that it is Jesus alone who can make sense of God. The strategy of the father of lies is to continue to keep the sons of Adam and the daughters of Eve intoxicated with the wine of actually giving no thought to God. Drunk with such a lie, people remain relentless in their pursuit of status, significance and beauty, whilst being oblivious to the truth that God has already given status, significance and beauty to them.

Conversely, when the truth of being made "in the image of God" is grasped by anyone, that person may begin to experience the dawning joy of an inner contentment, of actually being comfortable in their own skin. Because, freely and daily they can begin to celebrate their inborn worth and intrinsic value as given by God and not as something to be grasped or earned. Indeed, in the words of the most authentic human being, Jesus,

"You are blessed when you are content with just who you are –

no more, no less. That is the moment you find yourselves proud owners of everything that can't be bought." (Matthew 5:7 The Message)

Fundamental to the recovery of who we were meant to be is that we are (as the sign on the building site proclaims) "Under Construction". This insight resonates with Paul's understanding of salvation, in that it is utterly comprehensive in its outworking. The salvation act can be likened to a well-crafted story: it has a beginning, middle and a definite conclusion. This is patently clear from the following verbs tucked away in Paul's correspondence to the early Christian communities:

"...you have been saved..." (Ephesians 2:8)
"...who are being saved..." (1 Corinthians 1:18)
"...we will be saved..." (Romans 5:10)

Each aspect of the grammar comprehensively depicts the scope of salvation as spanning the past, embracing the present and finalising the future. In other words, all of our yesterdays, all of our todays and all of our tomorrows are competently taken care of in the scarred hands of Jesus, the *Omni-Competent One*. And this is precisely the reason why Paul writes with glowing confidence to the Christian community in Philippi that,

"There has never been the slightest doubt in my mind that the God who started this great work in you would keep at it and bring it to a flourishing finish on the day Christ Jesus appears." (Philippians 1:6 The Message)

So it is that when we give our fallen selves back to God, not only does God accept us, but also in exchange, we actually find ourselves for the first time. Without God, many people construct, devise and conceive all manner of identities in order to conceal their deepest shame and darkest secrets. Their emotional skeletons continue to torment and bind them to the stench of death. People are afraid and daunted at the prospect of having to face their unvarnished and unobserved selves.

Before God, however, I am who I am warts and all, window dressing is completely out of the question. For what cannot be achieved with our own heroic willpower, Jesus has committed Himself to – the long haul of making us "to be our true selves, our child-of-God selves." Becoming our true selves, in fact, activates the process of enabling us to become more attentive to the need for greater candour in our private life. In other words, every attempt on our part to return to the place of being *"addicted to denial and illusion, hating God's light and being unwilling to come near, fearing a painful exposure,"* (John 3:20 The Message) will always jeopardize the ongoing saving activity of God to continue in our lives.

Critical, therefore, to the making of our true selves is our great need to understand that it is neither automatic nor the total responsibility of God. Rather, it is entirely contingent upon one very significant factor: our consent. For me personally, this is absolutely astonishing. Even though there has been great clamour in theological halls over this matter, God nevertheless had chosen to give to each of us the capacity to choose. Imagine this:

God is endeavouring to expand our freedom. Every moment, God is trying to make the capacity of choice more alive for us and clearer in us – so that we may learn that nothing is ever wasted.

Rather brilliantly, the seventeenth century philosopher Blaise Pascal captured the wonder of this amazing gift of the freedom to choose. He spoke about "the dignity of causality".[8] In order to better grasp what Pascal articulated, the best context is none other than the activity of prayer. When a follower of Jesus prays, God is giving away to them the unspeakable privilege of partnering with Him in fulfilling His purposes in the world. In prayer, they are joining the living God in bringing about the realisation of His heart's desire for the world. Have you ever thought just how breathtaking this really is?

- Have you ever thought that Pascal's "dignity of causality" actually confronts us with the insight, that the "movers and shakers" of history might actually be those who pray?
- Is this also why Jesus instructed His followers, *"to pray consistently and never quit"*? (Luke 18:1 The Message)

In other words, rather than succumb to the prevailing voices of the world, the followers of Jesus are those whose lives are "shaken and moved" by God. The interaction between the sovereignty of God and the prayers of His people must be viewed as part of the ultimate mystery of the universe. God has actually invited us to share with Him as He works attentively to release us from our self-preoccupation, in order to be increasingly God pre-occupied in the transformation of the world.

The rationale for this is because our inner nature is absolutely predisposed to serving self. God wants to and has to change our inner nature if we are to reflect what is entirely true of His nature – that He is utterly and generously self-giving. This is love in its purest and most powerful sense.

An anthropologist was confronted with a startling revelation when he spent some time with the Hopi people, one of the oldest, indigenous tribes in America. He noticed the dominance of the rain theme in the art and music of the Hopi people. He sat with a tribal elder keen to know why so many of his people's songs dealt with rain. The Hopi elder's response was simply, "Water is so scarce in the land where they live." The Hopi leader asked the anthropologist, "Is that why so many of your songs are about love?"[9]

Music composers and poets the world over, all know that the world of the human heart craves for a love song. Perhaps this is why so much has been written and sung about love in every known language. However, a love song in and of itself cannot effectively heal the human heart of its deep bias towards itself. The human heart requires a healer.

Basic to, yet not exclusively, the word "salvation" conveys the idea of health. The best news ever heard and far surpassing the greatest love songs ever written, is that the Healer has come and His name is Jesus. The world surely needs composers and poets. However, they only got it partially right with "What the world needs now is love..." What the world desperately needs is so much more than that. It needs lovers who can give God's healing love away. It needs lovers abandoned to Jesus; lovers inebriated with this powerful love which transforms and empowers people to live life loved, the way that God has always intended.

"If I am a disciple of Jesus that means that I am with him to learn from Him how to be like Him."[10]

In my own faith journey with God, unreserved abandonment can only ever begin when a person embraces vulnerability, transparency and responsibility. These three words may be translated as the currency of the Kingdom of God. They are like the coin of the realm. God-lovers seek to spend their lives dispensing the wealth of His love to others. This *agape* is for the world of people. This love values the sanctity of life and also upholds a sacred view of all creation. God's love is a constant.

Without a shadow of doubt, this fourth attribute, that Jesus is Omni-Competent, takes on a larger than life meaning. Jesus' command, *"Come, follow Me and I will make you..."* (Mark 1:17 The Message) actualizes what is essential in our becoming our "true selves".

As we begin to walk with Jesus, then the Spirit of God is able to work with us and bring to us on a daily, moment by moment basis, the efficacy of Jesus' saving activity accomplished at the cross and resurrection. Jesus' command, "Come, follow Me and I will make you..." actually reinforces the fact that salvation and discipleship are inextricably connected. However, when the lines between salvation and discipleship are blurred, we can lose sight of the comprehensive nature of the saving activity of God. Yes, we begin with a decision to be saved from our enslavement to our fallen selves, but we must also diligently continue on in our faith journey in order to be saved into our true child of God selves.

What we are becoming is a mystery and what we already are in Christ is a miracle.

There is both simplicity and profundity. Basic to being a true disciple of Jesus is keeping in step with His Spirit. It is not merely and only about the acquisition of knowledge and mastering the art of memorisation of scriptures, or being consistently consistent in all things spiritual. The outworking of salvation, keeping in step with the Spirit, is intended to be overwhelmingly transformative and radically empowering of a life which reflects the genuine article of being truly human. Dallas Willard says that Jesus called us,

"...not to do what he did, but to be as he was, permeated with love. Then the doing of what he did and said becomes the natural expression of who we are in him."[11]

When it comes to the notion of losing our salvation *this can be reduced to giving up following Jesus*. In other words, we choose to live life on our terms. We choose to stop walking with Him. We hurl back into Jesus' face His gift of unconditional love and His zealous commitment to work with us and change us from the inside out. By throwing the decision which we had made to follow Jesus back in His face, we are effectively forfeiting the rich opportunity of allowing Jesus to make us, "to be our true selves, our child-of-God selves." Gary Thomas insightfully reinforces this assertion by suggesting that,

"The biggest block to our surrender is not our appetites and wayward desires but our addiction to running our lives."[12]

Therefore, the comprehensive nature of salvation must always be viewed as a response to Jesus' imperative "Come follow Me...". As we consciously, daily choose to follow Him, it is only then that we are able to celebrate His unrelenting love and His unswerving commitment to make us to become our true child of God selves.

Why then are vulnerability, transparency and responsibility so significant in this journey of becoming our true child of God selves?

In the Christian tradition, without a second guess the Church would declare that God is all powerful. However, it would always be with some degree of reticence and qualification to align God with the language of vulnerability, transparency and responsibility. We have no apparent difficulty in being able to rationalise their significance in relation to Jesus the Nazarene. As a human being He displayed these attributes in His public life and mission. On the other hand, what is often left out of this equation is that Jesus is none other than God. Jesus knows who He is and where He is going, and yet, it is Jesus as God who supremely embodies vulnerability, transparency and responsibility.

How disturbing the first century world must have been for Jesus.

He found Himself among a people whose history and tradition had so shaped their thinking about who God was and how God was supposed to behave that they actually did not see God coming. In fact, when Jesus arrived it was the educated and the informed who kept Him at arm's length. With a touch of wit one could say that perhaps the acceptable practice of keeping God at bay belongs to the rather arrogant nation of Absurdistan! If this were not so serious, we would be tempted to laugh out loud. Poignantly, the apostle John records,

"He was in the world,
the world was there through him,
and yet the world didn't even notice.
He came to his own people,
but they didn't want him." (John 1:10-11 The Message)

Whether it was in the first century Mediterranean world or in the twenty-first century, meeting Jesus the Nazarene for the first time is an encounter with the unfamiliar. Jesus would never allow His audience to settle down with any truncated and tidy explanation as to who God is. God is sometimes hidden, silent, absent, unresponsive and yet paradoxically powerful in suffering and whole in woundedness. God is beyond us and refuses all our manufactured labels.

Suddenly it came together, those three words - vulnerability, transparency and responsibility actually allow us to see not only the God who *made us* but also the God who became *one of us*. In the New Testament both Paul and John provide windows so that we can see God is both all-powerful and yet concedes to be vulnerable, transparent and responsible.

Our first window is from Paul's correspondence to the Christian community in Philippi. This passage is a favourite for many of the followers of Jesus. It offers such a magnificent portrayal of Jesus. Without overstating the obvious, the portrait we encounter is Jesus as God:

"Your attitude should be the same as that of Christ Jesus. Who, being in very nature God, did not consider equality with God something to be grasped, but made himself nothing [he empties himself] *taking the very nature of a servant, being made in human likeness. And being found in appearance as a man, He humbled himself and became obedient to death – even death on a cross."* (Philippians 2:5-8)

Our first observation is that Paul does not qualify what Jesus chooses to empty Himself of. Nonetheless, Paul is quite adamant about Jesus' act of self-disclosure and according to Paul, this is done with absolute, unwavering freedom. Consider Paul's portrayal:

- Jesus comes neither to earn nor warrant a reputation
- Jesus knew all the pitfalls and the pain of popularity
- Jesus does not find becoming a servant an act of humiliation
- Jesus knows that this is consistent with the very nature of God
- God constantly serves and gives to His creation
- Jesus does not find becoming a human being an act of humiliation
- God's intention has always been that humanity reflects His image and glory

Through this window the climactic moment for God to be seen as God occurs in a most confronting and astonishing revelation:

it is Jesus' unreserved act of obedience to death itself. This is precisely where Jesus chooses to demonstrate what it means to be vulnerable, transparent and responsible. Quite specifically, these words find their true definition in Paul's use of the verb *"humbled himself"* - God dies!

This is an abhorrent act of humiliation for God. God submits to death. In Jesus' willingness to become a vulnerable, transparent and responsible human being we encounter the quintessential revelation of what it means to be God and thoroughly human. This is the God whom Christians worship and witness to all over the globe. Similarly, Jesus is the genuine human being through whom incarnation finds the most memorable and lasting revelation of who God is and who we are.

This text from Philippians underscores the greatest and most amazing demonstration of self-disclosure. It must not and cannot be viewed as a one off act of heroism. As has been stated, the very nature of God is love. Inherent in this love is nothing more, nothing less and nothing else but surrender. In this very act of surrender to death, all that Adam and Eve had bequeathed to all their descendants is now fundamentally reversed.

Hence, the legacy of self-enclosure which had ultimately consigned all of us to deception, denial and death, has now been overturned. Because of Jesus' unreserved act of obedience to death as God, the legacy of death has been cancelled once and for all. Good Friday must be seen therefore as God's day of entry into the hurt and hate of the world, His day of bottomless weakness where the world has seen God – saw Him as Jesus connected in its deepest disorder.

This is precisely why resurrection must occur for Jesus. He is set deep in the jaws of death, yet He is not held – otherwise death would have the last word over every human being since Adam and

Eve. Whether it is the language of Paul or John within the New Testament, it is essentially the same powerful theme:

"Then the saying will come true: Death swallowed up by triumphant Life! Who got the last word, oh, Death? Oh, Death, who's afraid of you now?" (1 Corinthians 15:54-55 The Message)

"Because I'm alive you are about to come alive." (John 14:19 The Message)

Therefore, in acceptance of Jesus' death on our behalf, death no longer has the last word in our lives. With God's act of self-disclosure in Jesus, He calls us out of our places of *incarceration* into the new place of *incarnation*. So that for every person who wants Jesus and *"who believed he was who he claimed and would do what he had said, He made to be their true selves, their child of God selves"* (John 1:12-13 The Message). Our responsibility, therefore, to God and to the world of humanity which He so loves, is to allow the gift of our God-given identity to shine out of us. This is so that others may see, hear and experience the living God in their world. He has not abandoned it nor has He forsaken it. It is a world which God loves.

"This is how much God loved the world: He gave his Son, his one and only Son. And this is why: so that no one need be destroyed; by believing in him, anyone can have a whole and lasting life. God didn't go to all the trouble of sending his Son merely to point an accusing finger, telling the world how bad it was." (John 3:16-17 The Message)

David, the prolific composer of many poems, knew that *"heart* shattered lives hungry for love, don't escape God's notice" (Psalm 51:17 The Message). God continues to search for hearts willing to be manger scenes for His birth!

Our second window to peer through is the gospel of John 20:19-28. Again, those three words which God impressed upon me for my academic subject became all the more actualised. John invites his readers to catch a glimpse of one who is vulnerable, transparent and responsible. The disciples imagined Jesus as defeated and weak, and so they waited a day, two days, until the third day. And then, when it was evening...

"On that day, the first day of the week, and the doors of the house where the disciples had met were locked for fear of the Jews, Jesus came and stood among them and said, 'Peace be with you.' After he had said this, he showed them both his hands and his side. Then the disciples rejoiced when they saw the Lord." (John 20:19-20 NRSV)

The risen Jesus burst in upon them. He found the disciples locked up in isolation, walled in to their fears. He showed the disciples the wound marks on His hands and side. His first words are noticeably not condemnatory. Rather, they are affirmative words. Twice He mentions "peace" to them. Jesus comes to His disciples, not to bully or coerce. Jesus knows only too well how prone all His followers are to acting out the deeply entrenched script of self-enclosure. Concealment, invulnerability and irresponsibility are nothing new to the followers of Jesus. It is in this very awkward setting for His followers that Jesus then offers words of commission:

"Jesus said to them again, 'Peace be with you. As the Father has sent me, I also send you.' When he had said this, he breathed on

them and said to them, 'Receive the Holy Spirit. If you forgive the sins of any, their sins have been forgiven them; if you retain the sins of any, they are retained.'" (John 20:21-23)

On that first Easter when Jesus first appeared, one of the disciples was missing. This disciple's absence evoked an astonishing revelation in a way which would transform their vision of how they saw God and what it meant to be truly human. The transformative power of seeing Jesus could only be understood in Jesus' willingness in being vulnerable, transparent and responsible as both God and man with His followers.

"But Thomas (who was called the Twin), one of the twelve, was not with them when Jesus came. So the other disciples told him, 'We have seen the Lord!' But he said to them, 'Unless I see the mark of the nails in his hands, and put my finger in the mark of the nails and put my hand into His side, I will never believe." (John 20:24-25)

As the scene unfolds, now, at last, Thomas is in their company. It would not be at all difficult to imagine the disciples' enthusiasm. The boys would be competing for bragging rights. They were there; they had seen Jesus. Inconspicuous by his absence, Thomas had missed out on seeing and hearing the risen Jesus. One must keep in mind that Thomas was well known as the supreme sceptic, the doubter. Therefore, in his own words, he refused to believe what they had seen and heard. Rather emphatically, Thomas lets the disciples know that for him, it is not merely a matter of seeing the marks on Jesus' body, but he actually wants to touch those wounds. Unless this is made possible for the doubter, there is no way that Thomas will ever believe.

Quite significantly, we the readers are left with no doubts at all. The language of the verb is quite graphic. It is, *"Unless I thrust my finger and my hand into the place of those wounds, I will never believe!"*[13] What transpires is vulnerability, transparency and responsibility par excellence.

"A week later his disciples were again in the house and Thomas was with them. Although the doors were shut, Jesus came and stood among them and said, 'Peace be with you.' Then He said to Thomas, 'Put your finger here and see my hands. Reach out your hand, and put it into My side; and be not unbelieving, but believing.' Thomas answered and said to Him, 'My Lord and my God!'" (John 20:26-28)

Once more it is the first day of the week. Parallel to what had been previously mentioned in chapter 20:19-20, the disciples again find themselves in the same place. They are behind locked doors. Suddenly, the risen Jesus appears before them. Unexpectedly, without warning, the Nazarene interrupts them. Jesus stands before them. It is now the third time.

His greeting remains consistent: *"Peace be with you."* True to His character, Jesus offers no words of condemnation. Jesus comes to give Himself to Thomas. Quite literally this whole encounter is for the sake of one man, Thomas.

The operative word that governs this whole scene is "enclosure". Jesus followers were enclosed by walls of fear and Thomas must not escape our attention either. He too, was encased in unbelief. In case you may have missed it – *did you notice the absence of any reference to any of the disciples notifying Jesus of Thomas' absence?*

If Jesus was ever asked what it was that He contributed to His public ministry, His answer was resolute: *"I can't do a solitary thing on my own: I listen, then I decide..."* (John 5:30 The Message). In other words, Jesus came for Thomas because His Father told him to. In His first appearance, Jesus allowed the disciples to "see his scars". However, things were very different for Thomas. Thomas missed out the first time and so he asks for more – then he will be satisfied. Jesus has heard from His Father that Thomas wants to "see and touch".

So it is that Thomas is invited to touch Jesus' hands and side: "Go ahead, touch and feel the depth of my wounds." Here, Jesus models vulnerability, transparency and responsibility at its finest. Jesus comes not to offer an explanation to Thomas; Jesus comes to love Thomas. He comes as servant and saviour; as healer and helper; as pilgrim and friend. As we peer through this window, we are also offered an insight about ourselves which has the power to emphatically change our lives.

In effect, when someone lets you into their life through their wounds, this is when you can actually get to know them at the deepest level. Jesus and Thomas shared their wounds. This experience had allowed both Thomas and Jesus to know each other better than ever before. The gaping wounds of Jesus had become the point of revelation. Jesus had met Thomas at his most vulnerable place: his wounds were unbelief and doubt. This is further reinforced by the climactic moment of the gospel account.

"Unless I see the mark of the nails in his hands, and put my finger in the mark of the nails and put my hand into His side, I will never believe." (John 20:25)

Unquestionably, Thomas' name tag of "the doubter" would have to be removed. Jesus came for him. By being the God who is vulnerable, transparent and responsible, Jesus comes to all the Thomas' of this world. Indeed this is true for all of us, for all the sons of Adam and the daughters of Eve carry wounds. God is extremely vulnerable in His encounters with people. Even at great pain to His own person He will never coerce anyone to do His will. God is always responsible and transparent in His commitment to love a person without ulterior motive. God is light and in Him is no darkness at all. Jesus is the Wounded Healer.

Those three words, vulnerability, transparency and responsibility which God had given to me for the unit Patterns of Spiritual Formation found resonance in John's narrative of Jesus with Thomas. When authentic vulnerability, transparency and responsibility are modelled, therein begins the awkward rhythm of reciprocity in human and divine relations. Jesus had invited and allowed Thomas to enter into His wounds. By doing so, Thomas also invited and allowed Jesus to enter His wounds. Thomas, in fact, sees with new eyes. The mere sight of Jesus' wounds and the invitation to touch them transforms Thomas the supreme sceptic to Thomas the compelling confessor.

Fundamental, therefore, to any encounter with Jesus is moving from belief about Him to believing in Him. Mere abstract and propositional truth about God which demands the dotting of the i's and the crossing of the t's often fails to capture the sheer excitement and adventure of learning the awkward rhythms of relationship with Him. Every encounter and every incident involving Jesus throughout John's gospel culminates in Thomas' confession. Undoubtedly, this is where John has wanted to lead every reader of his story.[14] Thomas' confession is the greatest and highest theological confession found anywhere else in the New Testament concerning Jesus of Nazareth: *"My Lord and my God."*

What irony is this?

When we stammer about Jesus' identity, it is only to learn that it is our own unsettling before Him that wants naming. It is us who are in great need to become vulnerable, transparent and responsible before Him. Jesus waits patiently for us to allow Him to enter our wounds and come through our closed doors or high walls of self-enclosure. It is only as we open up our wounds to Jesus that we then consciously practice the art of not disappearing

Jesus' heart for the world is always self-disclosure. It is then that we are empowered and motivated by love to become vulnerable, transparent and responsible people in a world that needs to see Jesus in His followers. Just as the disciples had been drawn out of their workaday world of fishing, and out from behind their walls of self-enclosure, quite simply, and yet so profoundly, Jesus' command, "Come follow Me and I will make you..." was an invitation to much larger purposes than anyone could imagine. These are the words of Jesus the Omni-Competent One. They specifically suggest that *He will make you to become all that you were meant to be and to do what no one else but you will do.*

Do you recall the movie The Dead Poets Society?

It's the story of an English teacher's impact on a group of teenage boys. He arrives at Welton Academy, a stodgy prep school in Vermont, as an emergency mid-year hire. His first act as professor is to march his poetry class out of the classroom to the trophy case of Welton's proud history. Through the glass the young boys stare at photographs of former students, all with the same haircuts and dressed in the same uniforms. With their own reflections staring back at them, the teacher asks the haunting question, "Where are they now?"

"Feeding worms!" is the reply.

These once vibrant youths are now reduced to the dust of the earth. With that end in view, the professor whispers the Latin phrase, *Carpe diem! Carpe diem!* – Seize the day! Seize the day! In other words, if death shapes the future, wouldn't that very day be a good time to start living?

With that image seared in the students' minds, the professor begins to unlock new passions inside them to teach them how to live. One after another they step out of their comfort zones to risk themselves in the moment. Whether it is ripping out of their textbooks the chapter on Pritchard's rigorous rules of understanding poetry, risking romance with a girl from another league, or joining the secret Dead Poets Society, the boys all become united in their search for life in the moment. The reason is that they are forced to look into a future in which death has the final word; therefore their outlook on the present is markedly changed.

However, unlike John Keating the film's English teacher, a greater teacher, Jesus, would remind you, the reader of this book, to hear His whisper today in your hearts. It is so radically amazing: "*Carpe Futura! Carpe Futura!* – Seize the future! Seize the future!

Not unlike the students of Welton Academy, the followers of Jesus today also stand before the trophy case of the saints of Scripture and history. Their voice has not been one which has submitted to death as having the final say. They have not compromised their conviction and returned to the legacy of Adam and Eve. Scripts of self-enclosure have been cancelled. They have learned the new and awkward rhythm of self-disclosure and have seen Jesus, the God who models vulnerability, transparency and responsibility. Awash and ablaze with love they have been empowered to celebrate daily their true selves in God. So it is that they have found themselves for the first time comfortable in their own skin, knowing their true worth and dignity.

Without hesitation, I can say to you the reader: Carpe Diem

and Carpe Futura have become irresistibly and inextricably one. Their convergence has been actualised through Jesus' life, death and resurrection. He has caused the future to invade the present. Jesus Christ has had the last say on everything, not death! Therefore, in acquiring and practicing the skill involved in the art of not disappearing, it may simply be reduced to: *keep on allowing Jesus to go on making you...*

- Vulnerable – no more walls – no more hiding; no more pretending
- Transparent – no more masks – no more mere role playing; no more image-making in order to impress
- Responsible – no more excuses – no more blaming everyone else; no more letting someone else pick up the tab!

This is so that *you* may be yourself and go forward...

- resolutely determined to become a real person in a world hungry for the genuine and the authentic, and
- radically single-minded in realising that when Jesus said: *"I will make you to become all that you were meant to be and to do what no one else but you will do"* (John 1:12 paraphrase) is not for you alone.

There can be no more hiding; no more pretending and no more trying to impress others and, especially no more being irresponsible in seeking to blame others and letting them pick up the tab for you.

It is certainly one thing to allow Jesus to see our wounds, yet it is quite another to actually allow Him to touch them. Admittedly, to allow Jesus to see our wounds is a courageous step, and yet, it is the first of many in the art of not disappearing. When we begin with this first step towards Jesus we are actually honouring ourselves in His presence.

The really radical step, however, is when we go even further and allow Jesus to touch our wounds. It is then that we are saved from concealing our secret shame and secret scripts of self-enclosure; for Jesus is the best secret keeper of all.

The first step of being seen is to be generously applauded. Yet, to go further and choose to be vulnerable, transparent and responsible is to be receptive to love. Always be mindful that to be loved by God is perhaps the most difficult thing for a human being to receive. This love will not only never let you go, but it will also never let you get away with anything. God has always wanted to give you back your true self; the true child-of-God self which will allow you to just be yourself before the One who knows the very best and the very worst about you and yet, loves you all the more!

I cannot emphasize enough how amazingly radical the power of this love truly is. Neither do I wish to analyse nor theorize on this love. To do so would never effectively allow us capture its potency. Rather, I am so thoroughly convinced that love is power in the best and purest sense.

The reason for saying this is because it emanates from the source of the very One, namely God who is love (1 John 4:8). John's insight would have to be the most comprehensive and sublime of all the biblical affirmations of God's being. Basically, it means that at the core of all that God does is love. No matter how difficult it may be to grasp, the fountain from which all of God's activity originates is self-giving love. Ultimately, salvation is not the abandonment of our humanness, but a radical transformation into all that represents true humanness.

Finally, the closing chapter to this book Meeting God Face to

Face confronts us with the liberating truth, that even though in the Garden of Eden our first parents hid their faces from God, it was always God's intention to reveal His face to them and to us in order that all would be found.

The continuum occurs as He invites us to see His face in Jesus, from our own beginning right on through to the ending of our own unique story. However, a point of reflection...

In this Face is the love
That I'd always dreamed about
This is the love
That found me out.
You drew me and claimed me
And made me your very own
You held me and
calmed me
You made Yourself known.

I couldn't take it in
And I still struggle for breath
When I collapse and say
"I've got nothing left."
But you never ever turn away
You never ever leave
You stay with me and
beside me
You help me to breathe.
The exquisiteness of your beauty
The perfume of your love
The awe of your presence
Can never ever be enough.
(V. Shore, 2009)

Endnotes:

1. G. Wilkes and W. Krebs (consulting eds.), Collins Concise Dictionary (Sydney, Australia: HarperCollins, 3rd edition, 1995: 1515).

2. Refer to Walking on Water: Reflections on Faith and Art (Harold Shaw: 1980) p23.

3. Refer to T. Howard, Dove Descending: A Journey into the T. S. Eliot's Four Quartets: Little Gidding Sapientia Classics, (Ignatius Press: 2006), p129.

4. This is my paraphrase of Romans 5:5

5. F. Dostoyevsky, The Brothers Karamazov, trans. R. Pevear and L. Volokhonsky (New York: Random House, 1990) p44.

6. Dante's quote is cited by the Franciscan Father, Richard Rohr from Enneagram II: Advancing Spiritual Discernment. (Toronto Ontario, Canada: Enneagram North, 1995) p189.

7. John 8:44 for this rather telling expression from Jesus

8. Refer to Pensées (trans.), A. Krailsheimer, (New York: Penguin, 1966), p32.

9. Refer to Gregory MacNamee, Gila: The Life and Death of an American River (New York: Orion, 1994), p147-48.

10. Dallas Willard (1998:303)

11. Dallas Willard, The Divine Conspiracy (London: Fount Paperbacks, 1998) p204.

12. Refer to Seeking the Face of God (Eugene, Oregon: Harvest House, 1994) p91.

13. The verb conveys the same sense as Jesus being "thrust/driven" out by the Spirit into the wilderness (Mark 1:12); or Jesus' exhortation to His disciples to pray to the Lord to "thrust/drive" out workers into the harvest (Matthew 9:38). In all cases as with John 20:27 it is from the same word.

14. Through all that has preceded this incident, some nineteen chapters, replete with astonishing encounters with Jesus, John waits until the very end.

"In the end
that Face which is the delight or
the terror of the universe
must be turned upon each of us,
either with one expression or
with the other;
either conferring glory inexpressible or
inflicting shame
that can never be cured or disguised."
(C.S. Lewis, 1947)

5
Meeting God Face to Face

Unequivocally, it has been my intention all along to move you closer and further into the larger world of God. Admittedly, such a comment may be viewed as rather ambitious on my part. But from the very outset, the thesis of this book is based on the notion that it has always been God's intention that we would be "found" by Him. Therefore, all such ideas which erroneously propagate the message that God may be found by us can, I believe, spawn an inaccurate portrayal of what the Christian Scriptures evince.

It is true that the Scriptures do speak about the quest of seeking after God. Nevertheless, this must always be seen from the perspective that our seeking after God is driven at the outset by *His initiative*. And then, as we search, it is we who are found by God. "Being found" is foundational to the odyssey of true knowing. Inherent in true knowing are the seeds of double knowledge[1] – a knowing of God and a knowing of ourselves. It is precisely this dual aspect which reinforces what has been true all along – that each of us are meant to truly live in relationship, firstly with God the true knower and secondly with others.

The rationale behind this is that we might learn to live and not merely co-exist in some awkward, clumsy attempt at being human. Where true life is unmistakable one is fully present to the other. This is doubly true of what it means to know God and to be known by Him. It can never be merely a one-way street. This double knowledge is energised by the oil of reciprocity. God has made Himself known; it is in the unveiling of His face towards us. What is intrinsically true in the world of relationships is that in the face of another we can either be found or remain hidden to ourselves. For it is through the human face that each of us mirrors to one another an invitation to live life loved or, conversely, through our faces mirror a sense of alienation or estrangement. Thus we either remain estranged and distant as persons hiding behind our cleverly designed masks or we become increasingly fully human and fully alive to God and one another. We were meant to be truly found. King David reminds us of this mirroring:

"I sought the Lord, and He answered me and delivered me from all my fears. Those who look to Him are radiant with joy; their faces will never be ashamed." (Psalm 34:4-5 HCSB: 2010)

It is easy to understand why the face of a person would be radiant with joy who has been delivered from all their fears. What is apparent, however, is not merely this obvious conclusion. Joy is not about having a particular type of personality or temperament and always being buoyant and animated because everything has worked out well. Rather, it is a joy which is evident in the certainty that whether the day is long or the night very dark, God's face towards us is one of openness and His heart is fully accessible.

In other words, regardless of everything which life hurls at us, the God who has made Himself known delights to grace us with unfettered joy in Him. His purpose is that we may be empowered to live joyfully and not live out our human story stoically. Human faces were meant to radiate joy. And this can be known if we grasp the truth that life was always intended to be lived in one constant dialogue with God. Humanity can and must recover this truth.

This truth was brought home to me through the following observation. When we enter the world of the Old Testament and the New Testament we find ourselves confronted with a remarkable conundrum. A mere cursory glance enables us to recognise the fact that the worlds of the Old and New Testaments are quite different. This is not merely and only because of the obvious in terms of different cultures and different languages, but more importantly, the relationship of Israel and the early Church with God radically differs.

The conundrum we encounter relates very much to David's words of having faces which are no longer ashamed; faces which reflect the freedom to walk with dignity and openness before God and others. The rich realisation of this truth undergoes a major transformation from the words of David to the time we enter the world of the apostle Paul in the New Testament many centuries later. This transformative dimension was made clearer to me in relation to the people of God in the Old Testament narrative. It concerns the anguish and distress of soul felt when God chooses to turn His face away from His people and from His servants. It is reiterated in the language of the Psalms and some of the prophets:

"How long will You hide Your face from me?
Do not hide your face from me...
Don't reject us forever, why do you hide Your face and forget our

misery...
Why do you hide Your face from me?
I will wait for the Lord who is hiding His face from the house of
Jacob
In a surge of anger I hid My face from you...
Then they will cry out to the Lord but He will not answer them,
At that time He will hide His face from them..."[2]

What emerges as even more fascinating is that the very word "face" is often considered to be synonymous with "presence" and therefore is often translated in that way. Think for a moment when Adam and Eve hid from God's "presence" in the Garden of Eden.[3] The word presence could equally say "face". In effect, Adam and Eve hid their faces from God's face as He sought to find them. Moreover, there is another incident which caught my eye and it has to do with Moses in the Exodus narrative. Moses is appealing to God:

"Unless your presence goes with us, we shall not go up from here ... 'My Presence will go with you.'" (Exodus 33:12-15)

Let us read these words again in the interpretative framework of "face". Even though God has assured Moses that His face would be towards him, Moses is insistent that God stays true to what He has told His servant leader: "O God, unless Your Face is toward us we shall not move from here. We want to know that we have Your favour."

From Moses' perspective as the leader of Israel, in order for him to continue to lead this stubborn and rebellious brood, he demanded of God the assurance that God would also continue with him and His people. Moses knew that when God was with them – His *presence*, His *face* towards them – this would engender the assurance that God's favour was upon His people and therefore the journey ahead of them.

A person does not have to live too long to discover that in the world of human relationships there is absolutely nothing quite like the painful and very distressing experience when someone has turned their face away from you. Metaphorically, what this represents in the physical realm is a withdrawal of their presence. The experience is all the more intensified when it has to do with someone with whom we are very close and especially, someone who is also a very important and significant other to us. Perhaps it is a parent with his son or daughter; a husband with his wife; two intimate friends, and so the list goes on. We may well be able to identify with such a painful ordeal in the realm of human relationships.

How much more difficult is it when it comes to our relationship with God?

The sense of the heavens being likened to brass and God being somewhat remote and distant are certainly not unfamiliar. Think of what it would mean for Israel when God chose to hide His face, especially in light of the following text:

"Moses said to the LORD, You have been telling me, 'Lead these people, but you have not let me know whom you will send with me ... The LORD replied, 'My Presence will go with you...'" (Exodus 33:12-17)

This is surely the language of covenant. The Catholic scholar G.K. Chesterton rightly grasps the depth of the commitment which God entered into with His people in the realm of marriage:

"Every act of will is an act of self-limitation. To desire action is to desire limitation. In that sense every act is an act of self-sacrifice. When you choose anything, you reject everything else ... Every act is an irrevocable selection and exclusion. Just as when you marry one woman you give up all the others..."[4]

When it comes to the world of New Testament thought, there is the conspicuous absence of "God hiding his face". Furthermore, nowhere is it recorded of Jesus exhorting His disciples to *literally* "seek God's face". Something has radically changed. It is precisely this absence which calls forth the need to excavate a little deeper. Just as the Hebrew word for "face" conveyed the notion of "presence" among its varied nuances, so in the Greek language of the New Testament one word, a preposition, radically affects and affords us with a significant insight as to what has changed for the followers of Jesus as the people of God.

When John introduces his gospel with the opening words, *"In the beginning was the Word and the Word was with God, and the Word was God"* (John 1:1) it is that tiny Greek word *pros* (with) which captures my attention. This preposition was intended to depict and convey the message that Jesus the Word was facing *towards* God. According to John, from the very beginning Jesus was face to face and intimate with His Father. John continues in his opening introduction to his narrative,

"No one has ever seen God, not so much as a glimpse. This one-of-a-kind God expression, who exists at the very heart of the Father, has made Him plain as day." (John 1:18 The Message)

This is so much more than mere indulgence in semantics. There is something more going on in the world of God's Word. Just as John had chosen to use the preposition *with*, so it is that we also discover the apostle Paul employing the preposition in the fifth chapter of his epistle to the church at Rome. It is Paul's specific use of *with* which further affirms what is fundamentally different concerning the relationship of God and Christians in the New Testament. This will assist us in understanding why it is that now in the world of the New Testament, the language of seeking His face and God hiding His face is conspicuously absent. Paul writes,

"Having been justified by faith we have peace with God through our Lord Jesus Christ." (Romans 5:1)

When this verse is read in the context of the first eleven verses of this fifth chapter, Paul provides a litany of categories depicting the position of his readers before God. This list must also be viewed as fully representative of all humanity before God. Concerning the church at Rome and ourselves, we are to be viewed as...

- weak and powerless
- sinners, and
- enemies[5]

On the one hand, this human predicament quite keenly eradicates any notion of anyone being acceptable or good before God. Indeed, God would surely be justified in hiding His face from all humanity. However, we need to remind ourselves again that worshippers in the New Testament do not cry out to God, "Do not hide your face from us!" The very reason for this language being entirely absent is because the tiny preposition "with" addresses and illuminates our way out of the human predicament.

From both John and Paul's perspective it is necessary to grasp the following insight: John's use of "with" in the fourth gospel, confronts us with the stark reality that the very One who was face to face with God from the beginning has, through His living, dying and rising again, made accessible and available to us weak, powerless sinners and enemies of God a way of being able to face God. Paul has presented the challenge that we who once had our backs toward God, and were so deserving of His wrath, can now come to Him. In effect, God has revealed His face towards me in His Son, the Saviour Jesus. David's words find resonance even more lucidly in this New Testament world of Paul:

"I sought the Lord, and He answered me ... Those who look to Him are radiant with joy; their faces will never be ashamed." (Psalm 34:4-5 HCSB: 2010)

In other words, we can now look with faces unashamed. Paul writes with further assurance to the Christians in Rome asserting that if anyone is in Christ, *"therefore there is now no condemnation"* and therefore there is *"Nothing between us and God, our faces shining with the brightness of His face..."* (2 Corinthians 3:17). If this were not enough to get our head and hearts around, Paul continues with his audience,

"We find ourselves standing where we had always hoped we might stand – out in the wide open spaces of God's grace and glory, standing tall and shouting our praise." (Romans 5:2 The Message)

The awesome picture which Paul has painted for followers of Christ is that we are now to see ourselves as *standing and shouting praises*, not grovelling and cringing with cap in hand begging for an audience with God or fearful, wondering whether we even belong. Rather, with bold strokes, Paul's portrayal of us is that because of Christ we come with open faces towards God. We are found and we are free to be where God would have us to be: *in His presence with Him, standing tall.*

In order to further strengthen this claim concerning the radical turnaround of being able to actually face God, we can understand that the language of God hiding His face from us does not occur because God comprehensively dealt with this issue on the cross of Calvary.

I am utterly convinced that the cross is precisely the place where God had chosen to both reveal and hide His face. Think about it: Jesus has been enveloped in darkness. And yet, the Father's face is paradoxically both absent and present in Jesus. He who is the light of the world utters His words of anguish:

"Eloi, Eloi, leme sabachtini - "My God, my God, why have you forsaken me?" (Matthew 27:45-46)

In our search to understand these words of anguish, we need to ask, "Where does this expression occur in the Scriptures?" To find out, we turn back to the world of the Old Testament – but how far back must we go? The most obvious explanation is that Jesus is quoting the opening lines of Psalm 22:1. Admittedly, it is somewhat difficult to comprehend what exactly was going on in David's life to give voice to such a cry. But David's words vividly and graphically describe his own agony of mind and body.

However, with the eyes of faith I am thoroughly persuaded that David's words were crafted prophetically. The psalmist was seeing with the eyes of the Holy Spirit down through the corridors of time to centuries later, to the day when Messiah Jesus would express these words as His own. It is David, in the Spirit, offering an extraordinarily precise description of the last hours of Jesus on the cross.

This is one acceptable hypothesis. But I would like to suggest we look back much further, even thousands of years before David's cry; the day that a Father screamed out in anguish with the pain of a lost relationship with a son: *"Where are you? Where are you? Adam, where are you?"*[6]

God's cry of "where are you" is not primarily Him pleading with Adam, "Son, why have you forsaken me? Why have you abandoned me?" Rather it is the sound of the heart of God breaking over the loss of relationship. These are really God's words of anguish!

Since that fateful moment in time the sons of Adam and daughters of Eve have ventured far from God's heart, often with their fingers in their ears, unwilling to hear His voice, unwilling to receive His love, unwilling to surrender to Jesus. Adam's race continues to busy themselves in the art of disappearing.

If we have been able to get a handle on the depth of these words of anguish from God for His lost son, we will therefore never look at Good Friday in the same way again. Good Friday confronts us starkly with the blatant reminder of the Father's anguish for all lost sons and daughters who have hidden their faces from Him. And yet, something so radically changes everything. It is all because of Jesus. At the cross it is Jesus who now must embody these words of anguish.

- Jesus withstood the beatings and remained strong at mock trials
- Jesus watched in silence as those He loved ran away
- Jesus did not retaliate when the insults were hurled, nor did He scream when the nails pierced His hands.

Jesus' words of anguish on the cross were not merely a question; His words were also a prayer. Jesus, as the second Adam, echoes the cry from the desolation of Golgotha, the place of the Skull,

"My God, my God, where are you? My God, my God where are you?"

What this means is that the consequences of sin have quite literally come full circle from the Garden of Eden to Golgotha. The one thing that is essential to understand is that implicit in the question *Why* is a belief that someone exists who can hear and answer. Once we lose all hope that there is an ear to hear or a heart that is concerned, despair becomes absolute. At the very dark moment on the Friday we call Good, the Creator God poured out all of His hatred and anger for every lie ever told, every object ever coveted, every promise ever broken, every act of murder, every rape, every act of racism, every inhuman act we have imposed on each other for countless millennia, and placed it all on Jesus' shoulders. It all erupted on His only Son in this God-forsaken moment.

Never have words carried so much hurt. The despair is darker than the sky. The two who have been one are now two. Jesus, who had been with God for eternity is now alone. Jesus, the Son, the radiance of God's glory and the exact imprint of God's being is utterly abandoned. The unity is dissolved. Father and Son were relationally ripped apart for all that we had done to each other. When it was the darkest of all, God had hidden His face from His only Son. God the Father could not look on His Son, Jesus,

"For our sake, God made him to be sin, who knew no sin." (2 Corinthians 5:21)

He who was with God from the very beginning now experiences God's face concealed and yet, mysteriously revealed. Jesus was abandoned for a time for us, so that we would not be abandoned forever. He had allowed Himself to be abandoned to the Father's will, submitting Himself even to death on a cross. The mystery that breaks open is that this was not the end for Jesus. These final words of anguish which have been born out of the blackest and darkest of hours have given rise to His words of affirmation.

Did Jesus ever want to quit?

Yes indeed. Hours before the cross, we eavesdrop on Jesus:

"Now my soul is troubled and what should I say – 'Father save me from this hour?' No, it is for this reason that I have come to this hour. Father, glorify your name." (John 12:27-28)

Come a little further. Jesus did not want to drink the cup of God's wrath. He badly did not want to receive it. Jesus, at this point, was no hero figure marching boldly towards His oncoming fate. Here is Jesus in meltdown mode. He had looked into the darkness and seen the grinning faces of all the minions of dark forces in the world looking back at Him. And He begged and pleaded with His father not to bring Him to the point of going through with it. He prayed the prayer that He had taught His own followers to pray many days before: *"Lead us not into temptation and deliver us from the evil one..."* Gethsemane, therefore, has taken on fuller and greater dimensions as Golgotha's battleground. From one garden to another garden, each reflects unspeakable anguish which would ultimately lead to unimaginable triumph.

"If it could be at all possible, Father, take this cup from me." In that very moment of resignation, Jesus re-signs on the line: "Count me in Father; not what I want, but what you want Father." It is this expression which empowered Jesus to utter His final words of affirmation for all humanity, namely, *"It is finished."*

We may well ask the question, "What was finished?"

Allow me to offer the suggestion that the history-long plan of God's search and rescue mission for humanity was finished.

Jesus lived a life of perfect obedience. *"He always did what was pleasing to his Father"* (John 8:29). His blood had been poured out on the altar of the cross. The sacrifice had been made. The sting of death had been removed. It was all over. The writers of the New Testament comprehensively accede to this realisation:

"Through death Jesus might destroy the one who has the power of death, that is, the devil, and free those who all their lives were held in slavery by the fear of death." (Hebrews 2:14-15)

"Think of it! All sins forgiven, the slate wiped clean, the old arrest warrant cancelled and nailed to the cross of Christ. And, he stripped all the spiritual tyrants in the universe of their sham authority at the cross and marched them naked through the streets. His power extends over everything." (Colossians 2:11-15)

It is done, it is finished. The darkness has been dealt with. Satan and the reign of sin to enslave people to self-destructive behaviour has been broken decisively. The penalty of sin has been fully met in Jesus of Nazareth. His words of affirmation are simply one word in the Greek: *tetelestai,* meaning "it is finished" or simply "finished!" It has been written in such a way in the Greek that it effectively *communicates a past action with a present effect.* It is not simply past history, it continues to have an effect in the present. Whether in first century Palestine or on this day in the twenty-first century, what Jesus accomplished back then is still efficacious for any person who says,

"Jesus, You took my place, forgave my sin, and restored me to God so that I can now call him Father. Release me from keeping up appearances and plunge me into Your reality. Invade me with Your Spirit who is whole and holy. And cause me to live with my face ever open towards Your open Face."

In God's search and rescue plan, what Jesus' executioners had intended as humiliation and degradation, as an exhibition of disgrace for all the earth to see, God would use as the means of drawing all people to Himself: *"If I be lifted up, I will draw all people to myself"* (John 12:32). "It is finished, it is done" is not and can never be heard as a cry of defeat. In the poignant words of Max Lucado:

"Had Jesus' hands not been fastened down by nails I dare say that a triumphant fist would have punched the dark sky."[7]

From the days of Adam to the day which Christians call Good Friday, all the words of anguish which would erupt from people who felt they had been abandoned and had nowhere to turn were fully and comprehensively met in Jesus' word of affirmation – it is finished! It is His cry of accomplishment on our behalf.

At the cross, with total abandon, Jesus had thrown Himself into the unseen and unfelt arms of His Father. Faces were turned on that day - the Son to the Father and then the Father to the Son. Then, throughout the centuries, an unending procession of the sons of Adam and the daughters of Eve continue to turn their faces to Him to this present moment. Wonderfully, eyes continue to be opened, because faces are being turned toward the human face of God on the cross in the face of Jesus, the bruised and bleeding one.

Some time ago I had the delightful opportunity to visit Lincoln Cathedral in the North of England. It is an astonishing piece of architecture, an Anglican cathedral dating from around 1072. Tourists are more than welcome and on a daily basis there are throngs of crowds. I was amazed, however, that I could capture a wonderful moment of contemplation. During those brief moments, I reflected on a tradition within the Catholic Church called the Feast of the Holy Face of Jesus. It is a liturgical feast that is little known. The Church's Liturgy provides an opportunity to receive grace to seek the face of God in Christ.

In no time at all my thoughts turned to Mel Gibson's cinematic portrayal of some of the very graphic details of the sufferings of Christ in His passion. Gibson laboured long and hard to display the intense agony of the crucifixion scene. However, as the moments continued the glimpse that I caught of Jesus on the cross ushered in overwhelming awe and yet also dread. His face was barely recognisable, it was so disfigured, yet in it I also saw my soul.

His disfigurement was unquestionably related to my own disfigurement deep within. I could not retain this posture for very long, as much as I wanted to. God knew how very introspective I was. The overwhelming impression which I sustained on that day in Lincoln Cathedral was one of God intervening, by saying "No more self-examination, enough is enough." As I turned my eyes from my disfigurement of soul, the face of Jesus was transfigured.

Could it be that my disfigured soul would also be transfigured as I looked into His transfigured face?

If this was how I saw my soul, what would this mean for all sons of Adam and daughters of Eve?

In the face of such love, all disfigurement of soul and being can be transfigured into unparalleled beauty. I had been defeated by love, yet not conquered by it; rather, taken further into it. Its lyrics pushed me beyond reason. Its sonorous tones pervaded my soul. Its cadences located me home, beyond all my perceived safe places; to move my life beyond control and a future beyond despair. Nascent and embryonic, admittedly, yet newness was filling me to the full, till I was overflowing with rapture. I had also found myself fully responsive to the image of the outstretched arms of Jesus on the cross. This image would remain forever as God's eternal sign of, *"I love you."*

Soon my contemplation became seriously theologically oriented. My mind gravitated towards the fact that there was so much more going on with the Christ of the cross. God in Christ literally degraded Himself. The word "degrade" comes from the Latin and conveys the idea of a step down. Timothy Keller arrests our attention with the following words:

"The physical pain was nothing compared to the spiritual experience of cosmic abandonment. Christianity alone among the world religions claims that God became uniquely and fully human in Jesus Christ and therefore knows firsthand despair, rejection, loneliness, poverty, bereavement, torture, and imprisonment. On the cross he went beyond even the worst human suffering and experienced cosmic rejection and pain that exceeds ours as infinitely as his knowledge and power exceeds ours."[8]

What paradox is this?

The amazing irony of the cross is that He who was everything had everything taken away from Him. God took upon Himself, in His Son, Jesus, the sin of the entire world. God fully revealed and demonstrated the incomprehensible essence of His nature that He is love. Incomprehensible, because without the cost incurred by such depths of suffering and degradation, love among humans could potentially remain self-indulgent and narcissistic.

As I further reflected on the death of Jesus, I was acutely aware of the two symbols given by the early Christian community, namely, the bread and the cup. The eucharist or holy communion speaks volumes. The bread (His body) represents the unveiling of God's face towards you and me in the person of Jesus the Nazarene and the cup (His blood) signifies the once-for-all payment for every sin committed, every dumb choice, every act of selfishness - in our past, in our present and in our future. However, a question immediately arose within me:

How do you see God's Face?

If it is stern and angry then the clutter of painful memories in your personal history has continued to conspire against you; a conspiracy wrought by both the forces of darkness without and within. I mentioned from the very commencement of this book that it is singularly important to be honest with both the darkness and the light. If I were to continue to indulge myself in the art of disappearing or hiding, this predisposition of mind and heart would never allow me to see God's face as He had always intended. It would only perpetuate the notion that I would be prepared to live a life of self-enclosure and not self-disclosure. Continuing in this vein would only ever produce a very poor and shoddy imitation of the incarnational life which God wanted to reproduce in me. In the words of Eugene Peterson,

"God knew what He was doing from the very beginning. He decided from the outset to shape the lives of those who love Him along the same lines as the life of His Son. The Son stands first in the line of humanity He restored. We see what the original and intended shape of our lives there in Him." (Romans 8:29 The Message)

As much as that moment of contemplation on The Feast of the Holy Face of Jesus helped me to catch a glimpse of the costliness of our freedom from a life enslaved to sin and death, it also gave me a glimpse of the glory that will be fully and finally revealed. In the final chapter of the Apocalypse the angel showed to the apostle John the New Jerusalem and what trapped my attention were these words:

"No longer will be there any curse. The throne of God and of the Lamb will be in the city, and His servants will serve Him. They will see His face..." (Revelation 22:4)

At last, from the earliest days of Eden, the curses of Genesis 3 reached their climactic end in the Apocalypse of John.[9] Now access which had been denied since the expulsion in the Garden of Eden is resumed and God's face is seen. This is the destiny of everyone. If I, like John, had been caught in this staggering epiphany, I would immediately usher in the sound of celebration and strike up the band and rouse the choir. Not so for John, he had already reminded his hearers in the apocalypse that such an unveiling will also produce sombre and ominous tones:

"I watched while He ripped off the sixth seal: a bone jarring earthquake, sun turned black as ink, moon all bloody, stars falling out of the sky like figs shaken from a tree in a high wind, sky snapped shut like a book, islands and mountains sliding this way and that. And then pandemonium, everyone and his dog running for cover – kings, princes, generals, rich and strong, along with every commoner, slave or free. They hid in mountain caves and rocky dens, calling out to the mountains and rocks, 'Refuge! Hide us from the One seated on the throne and the wrath of the Lamb. The great Day of their wrath has come – who can stand it?'" (Revelation 6:12-17 The Message)

For God's people, to see His face denotes great reward. Nonetheless, juxtaposed with this notion of reward, there is undeniably retribution. In the words of C.S. Lewis:

"In the end that Face which is the delight or the terror of the universe must be turned upon each of us either with one expression or with the other, either conferring glory inexpressible or inflicting shame that can never be cured or disguised."[10]

Hence, the unveiling of the face of God demands a response. The good news or the gospel proclamation is that no human being has to wait or put it off until the final day to respond. The cross of Calvary is the place where the sacred encounters the sinful; where the holy confronts the unholy; where the light shines in the darkness; where the faces of shame and fear, rejection and overwhelming guilt are defeated by the face of amazing love and unconditional acceptance in Messiah Jesus. The cross radically overturns any idea as to how we may have conceived God to be for us.

Who would have thought that God would come as an uncredentialled Galilean rabbi to force us out of our neatly arranged patterns of security?

Who could have grasped that in learning the art of not disappearing that we could actually move out into dangerous places of newness and vulnerability where we actually fear to go? And we can and we must. In this life, as in the following text from John the apostle, we must appropriate the powerful truth for which we are called to live out:

"Look at how great a love the Father has given us that we should be called God's children. And we are! Dear friends, we are God's children now, and what we will be has not yet been fully revealed. We know that when He appears, we will be like Him because we will see Him as He is. And everyone who has this hope in Him purifies himself just as He is pure." (1 John 3:1-3)

What is both remarkable and breathtaking about these words is that *"what we will be has not yet been fully revealed".* In all our very awkward attempts in our present experience to discover the answer to "Who am I and what shall I become?" must be matched with, *"we see indistinctly, as in a mirror, but then face to face we will know fully, as we are fully known"* (1 Corinthians 13:12 HCSB).

Pertinent to these texts in our modern millennia, Postmodernism must not determine how we should live. Nor should technology define our existence. Similarly, Secularism is an anaemic attempt at trying to make sense of life without any reference to the One who is the Life.

As a follower of Jesus, I am utterly convinced that there is a great need to recover the riches inherent in theology. This wealth is ours. Whether it is articulated by Moses or Isaiah, John or Paul, clearly our Christian text affirms the unchangeable fact that our identity is not marketable as some sort of commodity. Rather, what we already are in the Face of Him who fully knows us and what we shall become is altogether a present reality, as we live our lives loving Jesus. Our riches are the currency of faith, hope and love. We have...

- A faith which is grounded in the certainty that God is far bigger than anything or anyone and so much more than a mere construct of human ingenuity
- A hope which is indisputably never subject to ecclesiastical change, sociological upheaval, economic rationalisation or political challenge
- And a love which transcends mere sentimentality, which is sourced in the knowledge that truth is a Person and not merely a collection of Ideological slogans nor philosophical maxims

Any notion therefore of attempting to find oneself without any reference to God will ultimately leave a person stranded in a cul-de-sac experience of life. This existence would be characterised by the rhythm of going round and round in circles and being seduced by the clichéd or the trivial.[11]

"To be in touch with everything there is to know of God, it is imperative to be focused on Christ, God's great mystery. All the richest treasures of wisdom and knowledge are embedded in that mystery and nowhere else. And we've been shown the mystery." (Colossians 2:2-3 The Message)

The mystery has been unveiled and the mystery continues to invite us to enter in and embrace all that has been made accessible and available. His face is turned toward us in unending love and unerring grace. And His arms are ever outstretched as His eternal signature of, *"I love you."*

Endnotes:

1. Refer to the mystical writings of Julian of Norwich and Teresa of Avila.

2. Refer to Psalms 27:9, 13:1; 30:7, 44:23-24, 51:9; Isa 8:17, 54:8; Mic 3:4.

3. Genesis 3:8. The Hebrew word for face is also used of expressions like the "surface of the waters" (Genesis 7:18). Even in current English idiom some might speak of the "face of the mirror", referring to its flat shiny surface.

4. G.K.Chesterton, "Orthodoxy" in The Collected Works of G.K.Chesterton Vol:1, (San Francisco: Ignatius, 1986) p243.

5. All three verses are found in Romans 5:6-10

6. The crafting of this thought came about through a robust conversation (2007) with Fred Grewe, who is an excellent exemplar of humility and compassion, a teacher and confidant. The questioning emerges from Genesis 3:9.

7. Max Lucado, No Wonder They Call Him Saviour (Oregon: Multnomah Press, 1986) p61.

8. T. Keller, The Reason for God: Belief in an Age of Skepticism (New York: Dutton, 2008) p30.

9. Especially Revelation 20

10. C. S Lewis, "The Weight of Glory" in The Weight of Glory and other Addresses (New York: Simon & Schuster, 1996) p34.

11. Isaac Watts made the following observation: "I seem to have been only a boy playing on the seashore, and diverting myself in now and then finding a smooth pebble or a prettier shell than ordinary. Whilst the great ocean of truth lay all undiscovered before me." (source unknown)

Conclusion

My once upon a time script, as well as for family members, has been gloriously transformed. God's deeper magic continues with unrelenting passion as I embrace the truth that once a Mephibosheth, I do not have to always remain disabled or disfigured by my own foolish and stubborn choices. Similarly, inborn worth and value is not something to compromise or sell off on the basis of mere performance in order to acquire value and worth. Our never-ending story is primarily about becoming our true self in Christ.

This evokes in me both mystery and sheer wonder at the miracle of God's unending love and forgiveness. I am immensely confident that even with all my contradictions as a saint and a sinner, I am whole in the eyes of He who believes in me and knows the very worst about me and yet, loves me all the more. To be skilled in the art of not disappearing involves not a fastidious legalistic stance of making oneself more religious. Rather, it is in being vigilant and diligent in our desire to know and be known by He whose love will never let me go and never allow me to get away with anything.

Every feeble attempt I make to run and hide, I know that I am merely reverting to where I came from and not where I am heading to. The future has decisively invaded the present through what Jesus accomplished in His death and resurrection. Therefore, it is a necessity that I nurture vulnerability, transparency and responsibility as qualities of a beautiful life without the need for window dressing. I offer a final exhortation and benediction to conclude.

On a recent visit to the United Kingdom, an elder at the church where I was ministering penned this in language which is congruent with the worlds of the Old Testament and the New Testament (thank you, Martin). It is true for all who obey His, "Come, follow Me" invitation:

"The Lord bless you and keep you,
The Lord has made His face shine upon you
  – *may you have the power to know it.*
The Lord is gracious to you
  – *may you fully receive it.*
The Lord has turned His face toward you
  – *may you have the capacity to see it.*
The Lord has given you His peace
  – *may you have the courage to inhabit it."*

Bibliography

G. Archer, The New American Standard Bible. Chicago: Moody Press, 1987.

Holman Christian Study Bible. Nashville: Holman Bible Publishers, 2003.

G. K. Chesterton, "Orthodoxy" in The Collected Works of G K Chesterton Vol: 1, San Francisco: Ignatius, 1986.

W. Clarke and W. Wright, (Eds.), The Plays and Sonnets of William Shakespeare. Volume Two, Chicago: University of Chicago, 1952.

F. Dostoyevsky, The Brothers Karamazov. (trans.), R. Pevear and L. Volokhonsky (New York: Random House, 1990).

J. Douglas, (ed.), The New Greek Interlinear/English New Testament: New Revised Standard Version. (trans.), R. Brown and P. Comfort, Illinois: Tyndale House, 1990.

T. Howard, Dove Descending: A Journey into T. S. Eliot's Four Quartets. Sapientia Classics, Ignatius Press, 2006.

J. Houston, The Transforming Power of Prayer. Colorado: NavPress, 1996.

B. Hamady citing Richrad Mouw "Exploring Deeper Magic," in Making Life Work: When Life is Working You or someone you love Oklahoma: Tate Publishers and Enterprises, 2008.

T. Keller, The Reason for God: Belief in an Age of Skepticism New York: Dutton, 2008.

M. L'Engle, Walking on Water: Reflections on Faith and Art. Harold Shaw, 1980.

C. S. Lewis, The Chronicles of Narnia. San Francisco: HarpersCollins, 1994.

_____ The Weight of Glory and Other Addresses New York: Simon &
Schuster, 1996.

M. Lucado, No Wonder They Call Him Saviour Oregon: Multnomah Press, 1986

G. MacNamee, Gila: The Life and Death of an American River New York: Orion, 1994.

A. Marshall, The New International Version: Interlinear Greek-English New Testament Grand Rapids: Zondervan, 1981.

B. Metzger, The New Revised Standard Version: With the Apocrypha Oxford: Oxford University Press, 1985.

B. Pascal, Pensées. (trans.), A. Krailsheimer, New York: Penguin, 1966.

E. Peterson, First and Second Samuel Louisville, Kentucky: Westminster John Knox Press, 1999.

_____The Message//Remix: The Bible In Contemporary Language Colorado: Alive Communications, 2003.

M. Proust, The Guermantes Way: in search of Lost Time. Christopher Prendergast, (ed.), (trans.), Mark Treharne, Gallimard, 1920, Volume 3.

R. Rohr, Enneagram1: Advancing Spiritual Discernment. Toronto, Ontario, Canada: Enneagram North, 1995.

A. Schmemann, The Life of the World New York: St. Vladmir's Press, 1998.

E. Seacy, (ed.), Awed to Heaven, Rooted in Earth: Prayers of Walter Brueggemann. Philadelphia: Augsburg Press, 2003.

G. Thomas, Seeking the Face of God. Oregon: Harvest, 1994.

H. Wansbrough, (ed.), The New Jerusalem Bible. New York: Doubleday, 1985.

D. Willard, The Divine Conspiracy London: Fount Paperbacks, 1998.

G. Wilkes and W. Krebs, (Consulting eds.), Collins Concise Dictionary. Sydney, Australia: HarperCollins, 3rd edition, 1995.

P. Yancey, Disappointment with God: Three questions no one asks aloud. Grand Rapids: Zondervan, 1992.

L. Zeigler, "Christianity or Feminism?" in W. Dembski and J. Richards (eds.) Unapologetic Apologetics: Meeting the Challenges of Theological Studies Downers Grove, Illinois: Intervarsity, 2008.

About the author

Vangjel Shore was the head of New Testament Studies in the Garden City College, Brisbane, Australia from 2003-2009. He has a Masters in Theology from the University of Queensland where he completed a PhD, "Ears to Hear in the Book of Revelation" in 2003. He has recently completed an extensive teaching ministry on the Gospels in the United Kingdom, Atlanta and Brasil in 2007.

Subsequently, in 2010, he has recently returned from a teaching and preaching ministry in the United Kingdom. He has also written a chapter entitled "The Titles of Jesus" under the supervision of Dr Mark Harding and Professor Alana Nobbs for the publication *The Content and Setting of the Gospel Tradition* by Eerdmans.

From 2009 he was appointed to the staff of Hillsong Brisbane Campus as Pastor of Spiritual Formation and in 2010 was involved in the Evening College Course as Co-Ordinator and Lecturer. He was also a sessional lecturer in New Testament Greek at the AlphaCrucis College in Brisbane.

Currently Vangjel and his wife live in Bangkok, where he is writing his second book *The Art of Not Gettting Lost on the Way Home.*